Folk Song
in
South Carolina

CHARLES W. JOYNER is associate professor of history at St. Andrews Presbyterian College, Laurinburg, North Carolina.

Folk Song
in
South Carolina

Charles W. Joyner

TRICENTENNIAL BOOKLET NUMBER 9

Published for the South Carolina Tricentennial Commission
by the University of South Carolina Press
Columbia, South Carolina

Foreword

It is obvious that the great wealth of folk song in South Carolina can only be hinted at in a study such as this. Certainly this booklet makes no pretense to completeness. The general neglect of the South Carolina folk song in recent decades, however, would seem to warrant publication of a survey of its development and forms together with a representative sampling of the songs themselves and a brief list of sources.

Unfortunately, whenever any specimens of oral tradition are committed to print, something is lost. In order to keep the examples of folk songs presented in this study as far from the literary museum as possible I have presented them with a minimum of editing. I have even gone so far, in some cases, as to *de-edit* them, that is, to remove such devices of written literature as punctuation marks, in order to help the reader approach this material in its proper atmosphere insofar as possible. Spoken or sung literature is naturally punctuated by line breaks. It is hoped that my omission of quotation marks within the songs will compel the kind of attention from readers that is expected of listeners.

I am deeply grateful to the National Endowment for the Humanities for a grant which financed part of the research from which this study was drawn. In addition to the many scholars whose works I have plundered at will, I wish to pay special tribute to the late James McBride Dabbs, whose emphasis on the oneness of Southern culture first influenced me to study folklore in relation to the culture; to Hayes Mizell, who first suggested that I undertake this particular project; and to George C. Rogers, Jr., and Robert K. Acker-

man, of the Tricentennial Publications Committee, for their
support of the project. I am also indebted to Norm Cohen
of the John Edwards Memorial Foundation, Archie Green
of the University of Illinois Institute of Industrial Relations,
and Joe Hickerson of the Library of Congress Folksong
Archive for help on various aspects of the project. I am
grateful to Mrs. Robert Spencer for typing the entire manuscript. I wish to express very special thanks to Jeannie and
Hannah, my wife and daughter, without whose love and
support this would never have been written. Finally, I wish
to dedicate this book to my mother and to the memory of
my father, who sang the first folk songs I ever heard.

Contents

CHAPTER ONE

The Importance
of Folk Music

There is an old folk saying: you cannot tell the depth of a well by the length of its pumphandle. Like the shadows cast upon the walls of Plato's cave, the pumphandle is but a reflection of an unseen reality. The material aspects of any society are always merely tangible reflections of its nonmaterial realities, that is to say, the beliefs and attitudes by which the members of that society have lived. Perhaps the most characteristic expression of a society's culture, and its most precious cultural heritage, is its folklore—the rich humor of the folk tales and the haunting cadences of the folk songs. John Wesley Work's famous comment on Negro folk songs, that "since they tell faithfully the Negro's innermost life, both intellectually and spiritually, they are the only true source of our history," would seem to be equally applicable to all folk culture.

Folk culture is distinguished from other types of culture by the element of tradition. The distinguished folklorist Richard M. Dorson has defined folklore as "the oral traditions channeled across the centuries through human mouths." In the process of transmission by oral tradition over the generations, a line of folk poetry or a phrase of folk music had to make itself memorable, or it was simply forgotten. It would seem to follow that what remains, after generations of weeding out all but the truly memorable, must be close to the cultural essence of the people.

Traditional folklore, rooted as it is in the real hungers, needs, and struggles of man, is a means of preserving the community's memorable experiences; of protesting—humorously, bitterly, or militantly—the hard life imposed by nature or by the inhumanity of some men towards other men; of making educational comments about manners and morals, the trivial and the transcendental in man's gropings for a life of meaning and dignity. Folksongs, legends, tall tales, folk speech, beliefs, riddles, ribald jokes, ballads, rhymes, fiddle tunes, and dance calls have served, and still serve, a variety of purposes in the Palmetto State. They admonish, lull to sleep, call to battle, ring with hope for the prisoner, threat for the jailer, joy for the lover, bitterness for the loser. Folklore tells of birth, childhood, wedlock, work, fun, murder, love (all kinds, shared, rejected, or betrayed), courting, complaint, celebration, melancholy, and joy. In short, folklore encompasses the entire culture.

South Carolina was born suddenly in a seventeenth-century wilderness, possessing neither cultural nor folk traditions to call its own. From the earliest settlement it drew from two heritages—that of the uprooted Europeans and that of the uprooted Africans. South Carolina was the meeting place for two very musical peoples. Thrown together in a strange, fierce land, folk from West Africa and folk from the British Isles shared their tunes and styles. The working materials for their folk music came out of the day-to-day experiences of the settlers in the New World, but the threads which tied it all together were imported from the Old World folklore storehouses. Out of the grafting of these Old World traditions onto the New World environment, and out of the swapping of songs, stories, and styles between the European immigrants and those from Africa, a new folklore emerged in South Carolina—a folklore with both an African and a European heritage, but as different from either as water is from hydrogen or oxygen.

Any study of South Carolina folk music is necessarily concerned with the folk music of both the white and black folk who have made up the population of the state. The strands of their folk music have intermingled over the generations. In this cultural exchange the blacks have been equal partners with the whites.

Although black people arrived in South Carolina in chains, they did not come culturally naked. Their customs, attitudes, basic assumptions, and folklore had all been shaped in a different environment. From the beginning of their sojourn, however, the uprooted Africans encountered a new cultural milieu, one in which much of their original culture no longer furnished adequate guides for adjusting to a vastly different life. Separated from fellow tribesmen and taught a new language, these African slaves were inducted both subtly and forcibly into the master's culture. In the Sea Islands, newly arrived Africans were assigned in groups to "reliable" slaves who initiated them into the ways of the plantation. Such a milieu would certainly exert strong pressures against the retention of the African culture. Much of what the slave could know of life was what he could learn from other slaves or from the example set by the white planters.

The chances that African cultural details could be remembered beyond a single lifetime under such conditions were slim; that they survived in such numbers and that they exerted such a profound influence on the folk culture of *both* races in South Carolina attests to the remarkable vitality of the folk culture of West Africa. But of course neither the British nor the African cultural traditions survived intact. No group of people removed from one environment to another can escape the influence of the new situation. It seems clear in retrospect that what happened was a process known as acculturation. The anthropologist Robert Redfield has defined acculturation as "those phenomena which result when groups of individuals having different cultures come into continuous firsthand contact, with subsequent changes in the original cultural patterns of either or both groups." In the encounter of uprooted Europeans and uprooted Africans in the South Carolina wilderness, cultural integration was achieved.

This cultural integration generally went unrecognized, partly because the development of the unconscious folk culture was proceeding rather counter to the development of the conscious society, and partly because students of the folk culture have misunderstood the origins of many of its elements. For example, many so-called Negro folk beliefs are actually British. The "ha'nts" and superstitions attributed to the black Southerner's "primitive" African heritage are in many cases more properly a part of his European heritage. It has been too often forgotten that many European settlers brought with them to South Carolina all sorts of superstitions and supernatural beliefs which affected their understanding of the cosmos. Demons, hags, and ghouls were widely believed in, not merely by the common folk, but by learned men as well, and lives were regulated by a whole host of signs, charms, and exorcisms.

Similarly, in his studies of Southern semantics, Cleanth Brooks finds many word pronunciations which are generally considered to be of African ancestry, such as "gwine" for "going" and "sebben" for "seven," to represent in fact archaic English forms. Brooks' discovery that in Alabama and Georgia dialects a number of forms previously considered Afro-American were actually older English forms, apparently taken by slaves from the white masters, would seem to hold true for South Carolina as well. This is not to say that Gullah can be traced in detail to English dialect speech, nor is it to give credence to the assertion that there are few survivals of African words in Gullah.

If it is true that many supposedly African elements in the folk culture are actually British, it is also true that many supposedly British elements are in reality of African ancestry. It is all too rarely recognized that such items in the common semantic storehouse as the words "yam," "cooter," "pinders," and "goobers" are New World survivals of African terms. In his comparative study of Gullah with the numerous Sudanese and Bantu dialects of West Africa, Lorenzo Dow Turner discovered not merely the acknowledged handful but thousands of African words still current in South Carolina. In addition, the high degree of homogeneity among the Sudanese and Bantu dialects enabled these uprooted Africans on South Carolina plantations to appropriate English words from their masters, but pour them into African speech molds, in the process creating linguistic forms which resemble structurally the African forms. The same process occurred in other cultural elements.

Another important reason for the failure to recognize to what extent the integration of folk cultures took place in South Carolina is that anthropologists and folklorists tended to concentrate their research on seeking the "purest" survivals of British or African traditions. Thus collectors of black folklore—spirituals and folk tales—concentrated their efforts in the Sea Islands, where black communities have remained most culturally isolated. For example, the striking retention of Africanisms in the Sea Islands is accounted for by the lack of contact between blacks and whites. On St. Helena Island there were roughly 2,000 blacks to some 200 whites. Under such circumstances, acculturation proceeded much more slowly than elsewhere. Likewise, collectors of the folklore of the whites, following in the wake of Cecil Sharp's bulging harvest of British folk songs in the Southern Appalachians have tended to concentrate upon highland areas, where in remote valleys, British ballads and songs have been discovered in a nearly "pure" state.

Nevertheless, this polarized concentration represents the preoccupation of the scholars, not of the indigenous folk. The southern folklorist Arthur Palmer Hudson has noted that the singing habit was widely diffused in the South as a whole, and that the folk songs sung over the South are generally the same, regardless of locality.

Between the Sea Islands and the highlands, black and

white South Carolinians have been swapping songs and
stories, superstitions, and singing styles for three centuries.
Singing style played an especially significant part in the
acculturation process. Ethnomusicologists have stressed the
importance of singing style in cultural dynamics. In the
interchange of tradition, Charles Seeger contends, "timeless
universal values inherent in diverse traditional styles of
performance . . . are ignored when the song is considered
apart from its singing, and partly or wholly lost when it is
sung in a style foreign to it." A sufficient change in singing
style, in fact, amounts to a change in song. Black South
Carolinians tended to retain the *style* of African music in
this process of acculturation, but tended to adopt the *forms*
of European music. White South Carolinians tended to re-
place British types of ornamentation of tunes with glissandi,
syncopation, and quarter tones, all deriving from African
influence. Together, the black and white folk of South
Carolina created a new folk music, a folk music neither
African nor European, but partaking of elements of both.

This is all another way of saying that all black South
Carolinians have a European heritage as well as an African
one, and that all white South Carolinians have an African
heritage as well as a European one. This mixing of folk
traditions, this cultural integration as it were, would seem
to be the most significant single factor in accounting for
the richness of South Carolina's folk heritage. The new
synthesis has not been a static product, but an evolving tradition. Tradition does not refer merely to the past but to
a sense of the past still alive in the present. Man can never
simply throw away his past and begin anew. William Faulk-
ner tells us that "the past is never dead. It's not even past."
Tradition cannot be cast off like an outworn garment. A
misunderstood tradition can, of course, seem ill-fitting and
uncomfortable. As T. S. Eliot notes in his essay, "Tradition and the Individual Talent," "if the only form of tradition, of handing down, consisted in following the ways of
the immediate generation before us in a blind or timid

adherence to its successes, 'tradition' should positively be discouraged." A proper understanding of the relation of the past to the present, however, can serve as a great source of strength. The man who knows where he came from has a better sense of direction, of where he is going and how to get there.

Tradition, then, is not merely a matter of time past or of time present, or even of both, but of *timelessness*. Tradition stretches back across the centuries to the dim recesses of prehistory, but tradition has not yet ceased to grow and to evolve. Nor has it abandoned anything along the way. Thus, it would seem that it is a sense of tradition that makes one most aware of his own place in time, that makes one most truly contemporary. And the tradition of South Carolina folk music, rooted as it is in the real hungers, needs, and struggles of our ancestors, and embodying as it does their ideals, problems, frustrations, and anxieties would seem to be among the choicest heritages of the state.

CHAPTER TWO

Ballads

In April 1670, after seven months at sea, not counting brief and unhappy stops at Kinsale (Ireland), Barbados, Bermuda, and Port Royal, nearly 150 British colonists came ashore at Albemarle Point on the west bank of the Ashley River. Nearly exhausted from their ordeal, they nevertheless set themselves optimistically to the task of planting the first British colony in what would become South Carolina. Their optimism was soon justified; the young colony grew rapidly. Within two years the population had grown to 406; by 1683 it had increased to 1,000; by 1721, to 19,600; and by 1740, to 59,000.

The growth of South Carolina coincided with the period in which the traditional British ballads had their greatest currency in oral circulation, and the men and women from England and Scotland who arrived in the seventeenth and eighteenth centuries brought with them a rich tradition of balladry. The ancient ballads, some of them maintained in oral circulation for centuries, were an important part of the folk heritage of the early British settlers.

Ballads brought from the British Isles have enjoyed a continuing vitality. The survival of a ballad seems to have had less to do with its environment than with the nature of the ballad itself. Unless it either reflected some universal behavior pattern or could be identified with an emotion which continued to be felt it did not survive. A ballad which was no longer relevant to the folk society was simply forgotten. Part of the importance of the ballad is that what a society finds relevant is an important clue to the essential nature of that society. Of the ballads known to have survived in South Carolina, the overwhelming majority were either tragic or romantic ballads.

While the survival of the ballad was mostly influenced by internal elements, the form which the ballad took was very much influenced by the new environment. In general British ballads fared as one should have expected them to. Of course minor verbal variations resulted from misunderstanding or failure of memory on the part of singers, and from singers' attempts to expand or improve on their stories. Ballads in the New World also tended to change their language and to acquire local references. In South Carolina, for example, "Lord Randal" became "McDonald" and "Poor Anzo"; Barbara Allen's Jemmy Grove became Sweet William or Sweet Willie or Johnny Green; and "The Gypsy Laddie" (Johnny Faa) became "Blackjack Davy."

If we examine closely the traditional British ballads collected in South Carolina, a larger and more significant pattern of alteration becomes apparent. All the ballads underwent marked changes as they adapted to new social and linguistic influences, particularly to the presence in large numbers of another race with a different musical tradition. That there was an interchange of music between the races is indicated by the fact that at least two variants of traditional British ballads have been collected from black South Carolinians. One was a version of "The Maid Freed from the Gallows" (Example 4). The other was the "Bobree Allin" version of "Bonny Barbara Allen" (Example 1).

As a general rule ballad stories tended to be rationalized in terms of the new culture. The supernatural tended to be discarded. Those ballads that depended on outmoded beliefs or practices either disappeared or went through radical change. The British ballad in South Carolina experienced the same kind of acculturation process that it underwent elsewhere in the New World. For example, there is a loss of supernatural elements in the South Carolina version of "Sir Hugh, or The Jew's Daughter" (Child 155), which relates the same medieval legend as Chaucer's "Prioress's Tale." In "The Two Playmates," the little boy no longer speaks miraculously after his murder, but before. Similarly, in "The House Carpenter" (Example 6), a South Carolina variant of "James Harris, or the Daemon Lover" (Child 243), the hero is no longer a ghost or the devil, but simply a cuckolding sailor.

Changing styles in song caused additions or deletions to some ballads, sometimes with damaging effect. In some cases so great was the change that the original point of the story was completely lost. For instance, compare the "McDonald" version of "Lord Randal" (Example 2) with the "Poor Anzo" version (Example 3). "McDonald" opens with a conversation between a young man and his mother, a conversation which reveals that he has been poisoned and is dying. We may conclude from the last stanza that his sweetheart has poisoned him, but just why she should have done so we are never told. The ballad tends to brush lightly over such explanatory material in order to concentrate on the climax.

As time went on, ballads in South Carolina became skeletonized; little but outline was left in some instances. More and more detail was dropped; singers subconsciously tended to forego exposition for climactic action. This process often resulted in an improved ballad by bringing more comprehension and unity to the song. "The Scarlet Tree," a South Carolina version of "The Maid Freed from the Gallows," has been reduced to little more than a formula. A girl (Or is it a boy? One cannot tell.) is about to be hanged. Why? By whom? We are not told. She asks the hangman to wait for a moment, because she believes she sees her father coming. Then she asks the father if he has brought her golden ball, which apparently will somehow bring about her release. He informs her that he has come to see her hanged. The same sequence is followed on through the family until her true-love comes. He has brought her golden ball and thus sets her free. Unlike most ballads "The Maid Freed from the Gallows" has survived in an elaborately detailed ancient version which relates the story of a girl kidnapped by corsairs or pirates and held for ransom. Her fruitless appeals to her various relatives are described in detail, as are her reactions to each rejection. Ultimately she is ransomed by her husband. Over the generations details were little by little discarded; ultimately only the dramatic pattern and the climax survive. The South Carolina version (Example 4) has gained in intensity by eliminating the early clutter of details and focusing on the emotional core—that even though her relatives reject her, her true-love is faithful.

Three types of ballads have been collected in South Carolina: (1) traditional ballads of England and Scotland—those analyzed by Francis James Child in *The English and Scottish Popular Ballads*; (2) broadside or stall ballads, those syllabized by G. Malcolm Laws, Jr., in *American Balladry from British Broadsides*, and (3) native American ballads similar in style and form to British traditional and broadside ballads—syllabized by Laws in *Native American Balladry*. Most modern ballad collectors arrange their findings according to the numbers assigned by Child and Laws to their examples. As in the rest of the country, the non-Child ballads outnumber the Child ballads in South Carolina folk song tradition.

The Child ballads constitute the oldest group of ballads in British tradition; and this treatment of subject matter, form, and narrative method is generally held as a norm against which to measure other ballads. Perhaps the most important characteristics of the traditional ballad are that it (1) focuses on climactic action, (2) emphasizes dramatic episode, without transition or explanations of preceding action, and (3) utilizes an impersonal narrative style. Most of the Child ballads focus on a single situation; the

action is generally compressed within a few hours. There
are exceptions, of course, as in the Murrells Inlet version
of "Young Beichan" (Example 5), in which the action is
spread over seven years. Even in "Lord Bateman," however,
the focus is on a single dramatic situation (or climactic
action) when the jailor's daughter who once rescued Lord
Bateman arrives at his palace in the very nick of time.

Since in any given ballad emphasis is on a dramatic episode, with no explanation of preceding action or transitions,
the development of the narrative has been described as
"leaping and lingering." The narrative is not presented as
a continuing sequence of happenings but as a series of rapid
flashes which leap over time and space and then linger for
several stanzas on those scenes which folk find colorful and
dramatic. Far from a defect, this lack of transition forces
the audience to supply what is missing, demanding its participation and consequently heightening the poetic effect.

"The House Carpenter" (Example 6), a South Carolina
version of "James Harris," is a good example. The identity
of the "old true love" who has returned saying "well met
well met" is not revealed. The conversation of the following two stanzas, however, gives us enough information to
begin to piece the background together.

Perhaps the most striking quality of the traditional ballads is their impersonality. This detachment, or ironic
understatement, is not so much a literary device as it is an
outlook on life. Stories involving stark tragedy or bloody
violence are narrated with no intrusion of sentiment, senti-
mentality, or didacticism. The most brutal or bloody detail
is told in the same casual, unconcerned manner as a piece
of exposition. Two South Carolina examples should suffice.
In "Little Matthew Groves" (Example 14), a variant of
"Little Musgrave and Lady Bernard" (Child 81), a duel to
the death is described as follows:

And very the first lick was Little Matty Grove's
He caused the blood to run
The very next lick was Lord Donald's
He drove Little Matty Grove to the floor

Note also the sequence of events in "Lord Thomas and Fair
Eleanor," a Charleston version of "Lord Thomas and Fair
Annet" (Child 73):

The Brown Girl she had a little pen-knife
Which was both long and sharp
And between the broad ribs and the short
She pierced Fair Eleanor's heart

O art thou blind Lord Thomas she cried
Or canst thou not plainly see
My own heart's blood run trickling down
Run trickling down to my knee

Lord Thomas he had a sword at his side
And as he walked up the hall
He cut the bride's head from her shoulders
And flung it against the wall

He placed the hilt against the ground
The point against his heart
So never three lovers together did meet
And sooner again did part

The sense of ironic detachment, the ultimate taking for
granted, regardless of action or circumstance, is heightened
by the understatement of the last two lines. Unrelieved by
comment, the action stands starker and more emphatic,
forcing the audience to become emotionally involved in its
own reconstruction of the scene. Editorial comment or explanation would relieve the horror.

We have already noted that all traditional folklore, including ballads, is handed down through the generations by
word-of-mouth. The central determinant of ballad characteristics is thus the human memory. Only what is memorable

is remembered; and what any group of people finds memorable tells us something of that people's essential nature. A
major factor in determining what is remembered and what
is forgotten in a folksong is what the singer understands to
be the "emotional core" of the song. Over the generations
those elements of a song which are closest to this emotional
core are the most likely to be remembered, and those which
are farthest from it are the most likely to be forgotten. If
we look at ballads in this fashion, forgetting would seem to
be a passive phenomenon. Elements of a song are not
always merely passively forgotten, however, but consciously
or unconsciously rejected. Entire sections of a song may be
eliminated because they seem ridiculous, or offensive, or
because they rub some psychological sore point. Sometimes
such losses are caused by individual preferences; more often
they reflect group or community attitudes.

One is struck in hearing ballads by the emotional effect
produced by the repetition of lines and phrases. Repetition
in the ballads is highly functional: it sets up an aura of
familiarity in a song which engages the audience's sympa-
thies; it establishes a feeling of incantation which encour-
ages the audience to identify vicariously; and perhaps most
significantly it serves as an aid to the singer's memory. The
most typical form of ballad repetition is called *incremental
repetition,* or "cumulative iteration," a device by which the
action is advanced by the recurrence of stanzas or groups of
stanzas with only a slight "increment" or addition or
change that advances the story or contributes more information, as, for instance, in "The Scarlet Tree" (Example
4). A particularly admirable illustration of incremental
repetition is seen in a South Carolina version of "Edward"
(Example 7).

In another example, "McDonald" (Example 2), each new
question and each new answer advances the dramatic dialogue one step further toward the revelation. These small
advances tend to lull the listener until the revelation of the
final stanza has a heightened impact. Incremental repetition

thus ties the elements of the story into a sense of wholeness
that helps counteract the disunity created by the leaping and
lingering technique.

Most of the American Child ballads fit clearly into one
of two structural patterns, which Roger Abrahams and
George Foss call the *morality* mode and *romance* mode.
Action in the morality mode is touched off by some violation
of law or taboo and is concluded when an appropriate
punishment is imposed. Many ballads in the morality mode
are concerned with murder and its consequences. For
instance, in "Lord Thomas," a Murrells Inlet version of
Child 73 (Example 8), the Brown Girl stabs Fair Ellen with
her little penknife, whereupon she is decapitated by Lord
Thomas, who then immediately commits suicide. The crime
and punishment theme clearly constitutes the emotional core
of the ballad.

In "Little Matty Groves" (Example 14) the violation is
adultery. The punishment, by death, is described more
graphically than any other element. "The House Carpenter"
(Example 6) is also concerned with an adulterous relationship which is punished by death, in this case by drowning.
An exception is "Andrew Bartin" a South Carolina ballad
with elements of Child 167, 250, and 287 (Example 9).
Bartin's violation is piracy, but unlike his English proto-
types he is unpunished at the end of the song. Contrast the
South Carolina ending with the pirate's fate in a British
version of the same ballad, "Henry Martyn."

> For three long hours they merrily fought
> For hours they fought full three
> At last a deep wound got Henry Martyn
> And down by the mast fell he

Action in the romance mode is set off by some feeling of
need or lack and is concluded by the elimination of that
lack. Most of the romance ballads start with the separation
of lovers and end in some kind of reunification. Male heroes
in the romance ballads, unlike their counterparts in me-

dieval romance, who initiate action and carry it through to a dramatic conclusion, are curiously docile or even immobilized. Lord Bateman (Example 5) is incarcerated in jail during the beginning of his romance, and after his escape he forgets his lover-accomplice. Similarly Barbara Allen's Sweet William is laid up in bed (Example 13). Such action as the hero initiates is usually to accomplish his separation from his beloved. Lord Lovel just rides away "strange countries for to see" (Example 11). Lord Thomas marries the Brown Girl rather than his true love (Example 8). George Collins has been out riding "last Wednesday night" with no explanation when he is taken ill.

Only in "The Maid Freed from the Gallows" does the male perform some positive act to save his beloved; however, in most American versions of the ballad the sex roles have been reversed, with the girl saving her lover. In "The Scarlet Tree," the South Carolina version (Example 4), the sex of neither the condemned nor the sweetheart is indicated in the song. This role reversal seems to be a typical development of the romantic pattern.

Even more typical, apparently, is the transformation of the romantic pattern from terms of life to terms of death. The lovers are separated as usual, but their reunion comes not in the marriage bed but in the shared grave. Lord Thomas and Fair Ellen find neither happiness nor fulfillment in love until their deaths; and even then the "other woman" joins them in the grave (Example 8). Likewise, Sweet William and Barbara Allen (Example 13), as well as Lord Lovel and Lady Nancy Bell, are reunited only in the grave. All three ballads feature, in most variants, the rosebrier ending. Lovers die, but from the grave of one springs a rose and from the other a brier, which ultimately twine together in a true-lover's knot. The device, partly ornamental and partly functional, softens the unhappy ending. Compare this ending in the following versions of "Barbara Allen," "Lord Thomas," and another version of "Lord Lovel," all collected in South Carolina.

They dug two graves in Steven's yard
They dug them side by side
In one they laid Johnnie Green
In the other Barbara Allen

On Johnnie Green's there sprang a rose
On Barbara's sprang a brier
They grew and they grew to mountains high
For they could go no higher
And there they tied in a true love knot
For all young maids to admire

They buried Fair Ellen beneath an oak tree
Lord Thomas beneath the church spire
And out of her bosom there grew a red rose
And out of her lover's a brier.

They grew and they grew till they reached the church top
They grew till they reached the church spire
And there they entwined in a true-lover's knot
For true-lovers all to admire

Lady Nancy was laid in St. Clement's churchyard
Lord Lovel was buried close by her
And out of her bosom there grew a red rose
And out of his backbone a brier.

In both modes death seems to be the solution to earthly
conflicts. Any possible action of the hero appears doomed,
particularly any action connected with love or sex. One
reason is the kind of relationship portrayed in the ballads
between authority-figures and young people who wish to
assert themselves. Expressed in family terms, the situation
is almost classically Freudian. Mothers oppose the love
matches of sons with other women, while fathers try to
frustrate their daughters' romantic dreams. Often the
authority-figures are merely older characters in the ballad,
but when this is true the young are even more brutally

defeated. In some of the ballads, for example, a woman cruelly butchers a young man with a knife, as in "Lowe Bonnie" (Example 12), a South Carolina version of "Young Hunting."

Much more mysterious is the father-figure in the ballads, usually a faceless symbol of power, sometimes appearing onstage only briefly, but making his presence strongly felt throughout any ballad in which he appears. Only a few heroes, such as Lord Bateman (Example 5), are ever able to triumph over the father-figure, and, when they do, more often than not it is not through their own action but through the aid of female duplicity.

Some ballads reveal an interesting emotional tie between the consoling mother and the young man wounded in love. In "McDonald," the drama is highly charged by the implicit comparison between the homicidal sweetheart and the comforting mother. Each stanza opens with a concerned question from the mother and an answer full of self-pity from the son. The nature of this mother-son relationship is suggested by the mother's murmured, "Whar have you been McDonald my son" and McDonald's weak reply, "Mother make my bed soon I'm a weary weary wanderer in a pain to lie down" (Example 2). In the great power struggle of the generation gap, the young men of the ballads seem to acquiesce docilely.

This docility, with its strongly masochistic overtones, is nowhere more clearly revealed than in "Barbara Allen." Sweet William, on his deathbed "for the love of Barbara Allen," summons her to his house where he receives her at his bedside. Plainly his aim is to arouse her pity and then be comforted by her. The strategem fails; they are united only in the grave.

In these ballads erotic love is explicitly rejected; sex does not lead to love but to sin, adultery, and certain death. Something is always introduced into the plot to accomplish its defeat—a fateful event, parental advice, or stubbornness on the part of one of the lovers, as in the case of "Little Musgrave and Lady Bernard."

Anti-eroticism in the ballads is not always portrayed in terms of tragedy. The farcical "An Old Man Came Tumbling Home," a South Carolina version of "Our Goodman," is as masochistic as "Little Matthew Groves" is sadistic (Example 15). The drunken old man is being cuckolded, but from his drunken docility we conclude that even though he understands what is happening to him, he does not have the manhood to object.

The drunken old man willingly and knowingly yields his role as a husband for that of a child. He once was a man but he has become, through alcohol, a child again. Not only does he fail to rise to a blatant challenge to his masculinity, but his questions are those of a foot-stamping child. His wife answers him as though he were little more than that. He sees through her act, as his sarcastic asides indicate, but he does not do anything about it.

Broadsides are fairly easily distinguishable from Child ballads by their more sensational plots, more subjective attitudes, more varied stanzaic forms, and less poetic language. The diction of the broadsides tends heavily toward stereotyping; for example, the "Come all ye" opening stanza is quite frequent. Broadsides might be likened to tabloid newspapers in their general style, method, and subject matter—love, fidelity, jealousy, adultery, incest, murder, theft, betrayal, pride, honor, courage, seduction, elopement, horror, rape. Broadside composers tended to plod through their stories grimly, milking every situation for maximum pathos. An interesting example of the British broadside is the Murrells Inlet version of "Mary on the Wild Moor" (Example 16).

On rare occasions the language of broadside ballads becomes inspired, as in the South Carolina version of "The Drowsy Sleeper" (Example 17). Like many fine traditional ballads, it begins in the middle of the story. The action is carried principally through dialogue. This version, like many American versions, has merged with the "climax of suicides" verses from the American ballad "Silver Dagger" (Laws G 21).

The most recent of the ballads are the native American ballads, dating principally from the second half of the nineteenth century and the first half of the twentieth. Quite similar in form and style to the British broadsides, including their situational stereotypes and many of their poetic flaws, the native American ballads lean heavily on scandals, tragedies, and current events for their subject matter, but with the American environment and history continuously adding new topics.

One favorite theme of ballad-makers for centuries has been the sinking of ships. A number of ballads commemorate the sinking of the *Titanic* on her maiden voyage in 1912, which had a powerful impact on the folk imagination. "Down With the Old Canoe" (Example 18) represents Dorsey Dixon's recomposition of an earlier version of the *Titanic* ballad.

Perhaps the favorite American ballad subject is the murder of an innocent young girl. An interesting example is the Murrells Inlet version of "Naomi Wise," sung to the tune of "How Firm a Foundation" (Example 19).

Some of the finest of the native American ballads from an artistic point of view come from black South Carolinians. Adapting the improvisatory tradition of African music to the forms and devices of English and Scottish balladry, black ballad-makers have been able to infuse their ballads with a spontaniety often lacking in others. A most complete version of "Delia" was collected by Chapman J. Milling from an itinerant black minstrel named Will Winn (Example 20).

The ballads of South Carolina are a record of social history. Most of them originated in the British Isles, and all of them are modeled on the patterns of British balladry. They are not, however, British. They changed as the lives of British settlers and their descendants changed. To understand the nature of those changes as they have evolved over the generations is to understand something very fundamental —the essential character of the folk of South Carolina.

EXAMPLE 1
Bobree Allin
(Child 84)

Communicated to Reed Smith in 1913. Informant unknown. The attempt to reproduce dialect typographically is
in the original. Reprinted by permission of the publishers
from Reed Smith, *South Carolina Ballads*, pp. 129–41 (Cambridge, Mass.: Harvard University Press, 1928).

In London town whar I were raised
Dar war a youth a-dwellin
He fell in love wid a pretty fair maid
Her name 'twar Bobree Allin

He co'ted her for seven long year
She said she would not marry
Poor Willie went home and war taking sick
And ve'y likely died

He sent out his waitin' boy
Wid a note for Bobree Allin
So close-ah she read so slow-ah she walked
Go tell him I'm a-comin'

She den step up into his room
An' stood an' looked upon him
He stretched to her his pale white hands
Oh won't you tell me howdy

Have you forgot de udder day
When we war in de pawlor
You drank you health to de gals aroun'
And slighted Bobree Allin

Oh no oh no my dear young miss
I think you is mistaking
Ef I drank my healt' to de gals aroun'
'Twas love for Bobree Allin

An' now I'm sick and ve'y sick
An' on my death-bed lyin'
One kiss or two from you my dear
Would take away dis dyin'

Dat kiss or two you will not git
Not if your heart was breakin'
You dassent drink to de gals aroun'
And slight Miss Bobree Allin

She walked across de field nex' day
An heard de birds a-singin'
An' every note it seemed to say
Hard-a-hearted Bobree Allin

She war walkin' cross de fiel nex' day
An' spied his pale corpse comin'
Oh lay him down upon de groun'
An' let me look upon him

As she war walkin' down de street
She heard de death-bells ringin'
An' every tone dey seem to say
Hard-a-hearted Bobree Allin

Oh fader fader dig-ah my grave
An' dig it long an' narrow
My true love he have died today
An' I must die tomorrow

Oh mudder mudder make-ah my s'roud
An' make it long an' narrow
Sweet Willie's died for de love of me
An' I mus' die tomorrow

Sweet Willie war buried in de new church-yard
An' Bobree Allin beside him
Outen his grave sprang a putty red nose
And Bobree Allin's a brier

Dey grew as high as de steeple top
An' couldn't grow no higher
An' den dey tied a true love knot
De sweet rose roun' de brier

EXAMPLE 2.
McDonald
(Child 12)

From C. E. Means, "A Singular Literary Survival," *The Outlook*, September 9, 1899, pp. 119-22. "McDonald" is described as a "poor buckra" ballad.

Whar have you been McDonald McDonald
Whar have you been McDonald my son
I have been out hunting
Mother make my bed soon
I'm a weary weary wanderer
In a pain to lie down

Whar are your greyhounds McDonald McDonald
Whar are your greyhounds McDonald my son
They are still out sunning
Mother make my bed soon
I'm a weary weary wanderer
In a pain to lie down

Whar did you get your dinner McDonald McDonald
Whar did you get your dinner McDonald my son
I dined with my sweetheart
Mother make my bed soon
I'm a weary weary wanderer
In a pain to lie down

What did you have for dinner McDonald McDonald
What did you have for dinner McDonald my son
We had white fish and poison
Mother make my bed soon
I'm a weary weary wanderer
In a pain to lie down

What will you will your father McDonald McDonald
What will you will your father McDonald my son
I will him my gold staff
Mother make my bed soon
I'm a weary weary wanderer
In a pain to lie down

What will you will your mother McDonald McDonald
What will you will your mother McDonald my son
I will her my gold watch
Mother make my bed soon
I'm a weary weary wanderer
In a pain to lie down

What will you will your sister McDonald McDonald
What will you will your sister McDonald my son
I will her my jewelry
Mother make my bed soon
I'm a weary weary wanderer
In a pain to lie down

What will you will your sweetheart McDonald McDonald
What will you will your sweetheart McDonald my son
I will her a keg of powder
To blow her sky-high
For I'm a weary weary wanderer
In a pain to lie down

EXAMPLE 3.
Poor Anzo
(Child 12)

Communicated by Mrs. John B. King, Williamston, 1913. Reed Smith said of this version of "Lord Randal," "Practically everything that could befall a ballad in oral tradition has happened to it. In this respect it deserves to rank as a classic." Reprinted by permission of the publishers from Reed Smith, *South Carolina Ballads*, pp. 101–4 (Cambridge, Mass.: Harvard University Press, 1928).

Where have you been poor Anzo my son
Where have you been poor Anzo my son
I have been out a-hunting make my bed soon
I am sick in my heart I should fail and lie down

What did you leave your dear father for Anzo my son
What did you leave your dear father for Anzo my son
He has six head of horses make my bed soon
I am sick in my heart I should fail and lie down

What did you leave your dear mother for Anzo my son
What did you leave your dear mother for Anzo my son
She has plenty of kitchen furniture make my bed soon
I am sick in my heart I should fail and lie down

What did you leave your dear sister for Anzo my son
What did you leave your dear sister for Anzo my son
She has . . . make my bed soon
I am sick in my heart I should fail and lie down

What did you leave your dear sweetheart for Anzo my son
What did you leave your dear sweetheart for Anzo my son
Here is a red-hot iron will broil a bone brown
She is the cause of my lying down

What will you have for supper poor Anzo my son
What will you have for supper poor Anzo my son
Make me a little breely broth soup
For I am sick in my heart I should fail and lie down

EXAMPLE 4.
The Scarlet Tree
(Child 95)

From the singing of a slave named Margaret, who belonged
to Rev. Paul Trapier, rector of St. Michael's Church,
Charleston, c. 1856. Communicated by W. R. Dehon, 1913.
Reprinted by permission of the publishers from Reed
Smith, *South Carolina Ballads*, pp. 146–47 (Cambridge,
Mass.: Harvard University Press, 1928).

Hangman Hangman hold your hand
A little longer still
I think I see my father coming
And he will set me free

Oh father father have you brought
My golden ball and come to set me free
Or have you come to see me hung
Upon the Scarlet Tree

I have not brought your golden ball
Or come to set you free
But I have come to see you hung
Upon the Scarlet Tree

(And so on with mother, brother, and sister. Finally the
true-love arrives.)

I have brought your golden ball
I come to set you free
I have not come to see you hung
Upon the Scarlet Tree

EXAMPLE 5.

Lord Bateman
(Child 53)

As sung by Minnie Floyd, Murrells Inlet, 1939. Recorded by John A. Lomax. Library of Congress. Transcribed by C. W. J.

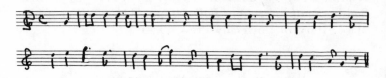

In India lived a noble Lord
His riches was beyond compare
He was the darling of his town
And of the estate the only heir

He had gold and he had silver
He had a house of high degree
He could never be contented
Until he crossed the roaring sea

He sailed east and he sailed west
He sailed till he came to the Turkish shore
They caught him there and put him in prison
Where he could see the light no more

For seven long months he lay lamenting
Lay lamenting in iron bands
Until he saw the rich young lady
That set him free from his iron bands

The jailor had one only daughter
She was a lady of high degree
She went unto the prison door
Thence Lord Bateman for to see

She stole her father's jailor key
And said Lord Bateman she'd set free
She went unto the prison door
And opened it without delay

Have you gold and have you silver
Have you a house of high degree
What would you give to a fair lady
If she'd from bondage set you free

I have gold and I have silver
I have a house of high degree
I'd give it all to a fair lady
If she'll from bondage set me free

It's not your gold nor your silver
Nor your house of high degree
All I want to make me happy
And all I crave is your body

Come then let us make a bargain
For seven long years it shall stand
If you won't wed no other woman
I won't wed no other man.

She stayed with her father till the time expired
Till seven long years was at an end
She packed up all her richest clothing
She said I'll go and see my friend

She wandered east and she wandered west
She wandered till she came to the Indian shore
She could never be contented
Until she had seen her love once more

She wandered till she came to Lord Bateman's palace
She knocked so loud upon the ring
There was none so ready to hear the fair lady
The brisk young porter let her in

Tell me is this Lord Bateman's palace
And is the Lord himself within
Oh yes oh yes my pretty fair lady
And his new bride just entered in

Tell him to send me an ounce of bread
And a bottle of his wine so strong
And ask if he's forgot the lady
That set him free from his iron bands

The porter ran in to his master
Bowed low down upon his knees
Arise arise you brisk young porter
And tell me what the matter is

There stands a lady at your gate
And she does weep most bitterly
I know she is as fine a creature
As I would wish mine eyes to see

She asks you to send her an ounce of bread
And a bottle of your wine so strong
And asks if you've forgot the lady
That set you free from your iron bands

He stomped his feet upon the floor
He broke his table in shivers three
Adieu Adieu to my new-wedded bride
This fair lady I'll go and see

Then up spoke his new bride's mother
She was a lady of high degree
Saying you have married my only daughter
But she is none the worse for you.

EXAMPLE 6.
The House Carpenter
(Child 243)

Communicated by Emma Clement, Spartanburg County, 1913. Reprinted by permission of the publishers from Reed Smith, *South Carolina Ballads*, pp. 151–55 (Cambridge, Mass.: Harvard University Press, 1928).

Well met well met my old true love
Well met well met once more
I have just returned from my old native home
And it's all for the sake of you

I could have married the king's daughter dear
I'm sure she would have married me
But I refused the crown of gold
And it's all for the sake of you

If you could have married the king's daughter dear
I'm sure you are to blame
For I've just married a house carpenter
And I think he's a nice young man

If you will forsake your house carpenter
And go along with me
I'll take you where the grass grows green
On the banks of the cedar-see

If I do forsake my house carpenter
And go along with you
What have you got to support me on
And to keep me from slavery

I have seven ships on the wide blue sea
All sailing for dry land
One hundred and thirty-six sea jolly men
And they are all at your command

They hadn't been gone more than two days
I'm sure it had not been three
Till she began to weep and mourn
And cry most pitifully

Are you weeping for my gold
Or a-weeping for my stores
Or a-weeping for your house carpenter
Whose face you'll see no more

I'm neither weeping for your gold
Nor neither for your stores
I'm weeping for my dear little babe
Whose face I'll see no more

Who will shoe it's little feet
And who will glove its hands
And who will kiss its rosy little lips
When I'm so far from land

Its father will shoe its little feet
And also glove its hands
And he will kiss its rosy little lips
When you're so far from land

They hadn't been gone more than three days
I'm sure it hadn't been four
Till there sprang a leak into the ship
And it sank for to rise no more

EXAMPLE 7.
Edward
(Child 13)

As sung by Clara Callahan, near Saluda. Reprinted by permission of the publishers from Dorothy Scarborough, *A Song Catcher in the Southern Mountains,* pp. 180–83 (New York, N. Y.: Columbia University Press, 1937).

How come that blood on your shirt sleeve
Oh dear love tell me
It is the blood of the old greyhound
That traced the fox for me me me
That traced the fox for me
It looks too pale for the old greyhound
That traced the fox for thee thee thee
That traced the fox for thee

How come that blood on your shirt sleeve
Oh dear love tell me
It is the blood of the old grey mare
That ploughed the field for me me me
That ploughed the field for me
It looks too pale for the old grey mare
That ploughed the field for thee thee thee
That ploughed the field for thee

33

How come that blood on your shirt sleeve
Oh dear love tell me
It is the blood of my brother-in-law
Who went away with me me me
Who went away with me

And it's what did you fall out about
Oh dear love tell me
About a little bit of a bush
That soon would have made a tree tree tree
That soon would have made a tree

And it's what will you do now my love
Oh dear love tell me
I'll set my foot in yonder ship
And I'll sail across the sea sea sea
And I'll sail across the sea

And it's when will you be back my love
Oh dear love tell me
When the sun sets yonder in a sycamore tree
And that will never be be be
And that will never be

EXAMPLE 8.
Lord Thomas
(Child 73)

As sung by Minnie Floyd, Murrells Inlet, July 12, 1937. Recorded by John A. Lomax. Library of Congress. Transcribed by C. W. J.

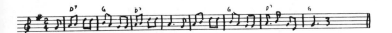

Come father come mother come riddle my riddle
Come riddle it all as one
Must I bring the Brown Girl or Fair Ellen
Or bring the Brown Girl home

The Brown Girl she has house and land
Fair Ellender she has none
I would advise you as a good mother
To bring the Brown Girl home

He dressed himself in mancerine (?)
The finest to be seen
And every city that he rode through
They took him to be some king

He rode till he came to Fair Ellender's door
He knocked so loud and strong
There was no one so ready to let him in
Fair Ellen come out herself

What news what news Lord Thomas she said
Are you bringing some news to me
I come to ask you to my wedding
Tomorrow it's to be

Come father come mother come riddle my riddle
Come riddle it all as one
Must I go to Lord Thomas's wedding
Or must I stay at home

I know that many will be your friends
And many will be your foes
I would advise you as a good mother
To stay at home with me

I know that many will be my friends
And many will be my foes
What care I for friends or foes
To Lord Thomas's wedding I'll go

She dressed herself in scarlet red
The finest to be seen
And every city that she rode through
They took her to be some queen

She rode till she came to Lord Thomas's door
She knocked so loud it rung
There was no one so ready to let her in
Lord Thomas come out himself

He took her by the lily-white hand
And led her through the hall
He set her down by his own sweet bride
At the head of the fair maids all

Is this your bride Lord Thomas she said
She looks so wonderful brown
You never had a fairer lady
As ever the sun shines on

This is my bride Lord Thomas said
This bride belongs to me
I love the end of your little finger
Better than her whole body

The Brown Girl had a little pen-knife
She whetted it keen and sharp
And this sharp knife she pierced Fair Ellen
And pierced her to her heart

What's the matter Fair Ellen he said
What makes you look so pale
You used to have that fresh a color
As ever the sun shines on

Are you deaf or are you dumb
Or can't you see to me
I think I feel my own heart's blood
Come trickling to my knee

He took the Brown girl by the hand
And led her through the hall
He pulled off his sword and cut her head off
And kicked it against the wall

Go dig my grave Lord Thomas said
Dig it both wide and deep
Bury Fair Ellender in my arms
And the Brown girl at my feet
Bury Fair Ellender in my arms
And the Brown Girl at my feet

EXAMPLE 9.
Andrew Bartin
(Child 167, 250, and 287)

From the singing of E. P. Alexander, Georgetown, December
11, 1904. Reprinted by permission of the publishers from
Reed Smith, *South Carolina Ballads*, pp. 156–58 (Cambridge, Mass.: Harvard University Press, 1928).

Three bold brothers of merrie Scotland
And three bold brothers were they
And they cast lots the one with the other
To see who should go robbing all o'er the salt sea
And they cast lots the one with the other
To see who should go robbing all o'er the salt sea

The lot it fell on Andrew Bartin
The youngest of the three
That he should go robbing all o'er the salt sea
To maintain his two brothers and he

He had not sailed but one long summer night
When daylight did appear
He saw a ship sailing far off and far round
At last she came sailing quite near

Who art who art says Andrew Bartin
Who art comes sailing so nigh
We are the rich merchants of merrie England
Just please for to let us pass by

Pass by pass by says Andrew Bartin
No no that never can be
Your ship and your cargo I will take away
And your brave men drown in the sea

38

Nor when this news reached merrie England
King George he wore the crown
That his ship and his cargo were taken away
And his brave men they were all drowned

Go build me a ship says Captain Charles Stewart
A ship both stout and sure
And if I don't fetch this Andrew Bartin
My life shall no longer endure

He had not sailed but one long summer night
When daylight did appear
He saw a ship sailing far off and far round
At last she came sailing quite near

Who art who art says Captain Charles Stewart
Who art comes sailing so nigh
We are the bold robbers of merrie Scotland
Just please for to let us pass by

Pass by pass by says Captain Charles Stewart
No no that never can be
Your ship and your cargo I will take away
And your brave men carry with me

Come on come on says Andrew Bartin
I value you not one pin
And though you are lined with good brass throughout
I'll show you I've fine steel within

Then they drew up a full broadside
And at each other let pour
They had not fought for three hours or more
When Captain Charles Stewart gave o'er

Go home go home says Andrew Bartin
And tell your king from me
That he may reign king of the merry dry land
But that I will be king of the sea

EXAMPLE 10.
George Collins
(Child 85)

From the singing of Annie Richardson, Murrells Inlet, 1937.
Recorded by John A. Lomax. Library of Congress. Transcribed by C. W. J.

George Collins rode home last Wednesday night
George Collins rode home I say
George Collins rode home last Wednesday night
Was taken sick and died

Mary was sitting in yonder room
A-sewing her silk so fine
But when she heard poor George was dead
She laid it all aside

She followed him low she followed him high
She followed him to his grave
She fell upon her poor bended knees
She weeped, she mourned she prayed

O daughter O daughter why do you so
So many young men a-standing round
O Mama O Mama it makes me weep
To think I've lost a friend

Take off take off the coffin lid
Fold in the sheet so fine
And let me kiss his cold clay lips
For I know he'll never kiss mine

40

EXAMPLE 11.
Lord Lovel
(Child 75)

As sung by Mrs. Norman McKeithan, Aberdeen, N.C., 1961.
Arthur Palmer Hudson Folksong Collection, University of
North Carolina, Chapel Hill. Mrs. McKeithan as a child
learned the ballad from her father in Charleston. Trans-
cribed by C.W.J. Used by permission of Arthur Palmer
Hudson.

Lord Lovel he stood at his castle gate
Combing his milk-white steed
When along came Lady Nancy Belle
To bid her lover good speed, speed speed
To bid her lover good speed

Oh where are you going Lord Lovel she cried
Oh where are you going cried she
I'm going a-traveling Lady Nancy Belle
Strange countries for to see see see
Strange countries for to see

And when will you be back Lord Lovel she cried
And when will you be back cried she
In a year and a half or two at the most
I'll return to Lady Nancy-cy-cy   (Nan-see-see-see)
I'll return to Lady Nancy   (Nan-sigh)

41

He hadn't been gone but a year and a day
Strange countries for to see
When a languishing rude came over his heart
I'll return to Lady Nancy-cy-cy
I'll return to Lady Nancy

He rode and he rode on his milk-white steed
Till he came to London Town
And there he heard St. Barney's bell
And the folks a-moaning around round round
And the folks a-moaning around

Oh what is the matter Lord Lovel he cried
Oh what is the matter cried he
The lord's daughter is dead a woman replied
And some call her Lady Nancy-cy-cy
And some call her Lady Nancy

Lady Nancy Belle she died today
Lord Lovel he died tomorrow
Lady Nancy Belle she died of grief
Lord Lovel he died of sor-row
Lord Lovel he died of sorrow

They placed him in the cold churchyard
But they put her in the choir
And out of her breast there grew a red rose
And out of his grew a brier brier brier
And out of his grew a brier

They grew and they grew to the church steeple top
And then they could grow no higher
There they twined in a true-lover's knot
For all good folks to admire-mire-mire
For all good folks to admire

EXAMPLE 12.
Lowe Bonnie
(Child 68)

As sung by Jimmie Tarleton, Chesterfield County, December 3, 1930. Columbia Recording No. 15763. Transcribed by C.W.J.

Lowe Bonnie Lowe Bonnie was a hunting young man
And a-hunting he did ride
With his hunting horn swung around his neck
And his broad sword by his side

He hunted 'till he came to his old true love
In a lightnin' he tangled at his reigns
No one was so ready but his old true love
To ride and say call in

Call in call in Lowe Bonnie she cried
And stay all night with me
A burning porridge you shall receive
And a drink of white chocolate tea

He says I will call in and I will sit down
But I haven't got a moment to stay
There's one little girl in this whole round town
That I love better than thee

Oh it's while he was sitting all on her lap
He was kissing her so sweet
A little pen knife was so keen and sharp
She wounded him so deep

43

Don't die don't die Lowe Bonnie she cried
Don't die don't die so soon
I sent for the doctors in the whole round town
For one who can heal your wounds

How can I live how can I live
You've wounded me so deep
I think I feel my own heart's blood
A-dropping on my feet

EXAMPLE 13.
Barbara Allen
(Child 84)

As sung by Minnie Floyd, Murrells Inlet, 1937. Recorded by John A. Lomax. Library of Congress. Transcribed by C.W.J.

Early early in the spring
When the green buds was a-swelling
Sweet William lies on his death bed
For the love of Barbara Allen

He sent his servant to the town
To the town where she was dwelling
My master says you must come near
If your name be Barbara Allen

Slowly slowly she got up
And slowly she went to him
Slowly she drew the curtains away
Young man I think you're dying

I'm low I'm low I'm low indeed
And death is with me dwelling
One kiss from you would comfort me
If your name be Barbara Allen

Don't you remember that long summer day
When you was at your table drinking
You treated the ladies all around
And slighted Barbara Allen

45

He turned his pale face to the wall
He turned his back upon her
Adieu adieu to the friends all around
Be kind to Barbara Allen

As she turned up for to go home
She heard death bells a-ringing
They rung so loud all through the town
Hard hearted Barbara Allen

She look-ed east she look-ed west
And saw his corpse a-coming
Lie me down lie me down on the lovely corpse
Let me have one more glimpse upon him

With scornful eye she look-ed on
Her cheeks with mouth a-swelling
While the rest of the ladies cried all around
Hard-hearted Barbara Allen

The more she looked the more she grieved
Till she busted out a-crying
Oh take you away and put him in his grave
For now I am a-dying

Dear mother fix my bed she said
Fix it so high and narrow
Sweet William died for the love of me
And I must die for sorrow

Sweet William was buried at his church door
And her a little piece further
And out of his grave there sprang a red rose
And out of her a brier

They growed up high on his church door
And they could not grow no higher
They met and tied in a true-love knot
The red rose round the brier

EXAMPLE 14.
Little Matthew Groves
(Child 81)

A collated text from two fragments in *South Carolina Ballads*. Stanzas 1, 2, 4. 3–4, 5, 6, 7. 1–2, 8, and 9 communicated by Tressie Pierce, Columbia, 1925. Stanzas 3, 4. 1–2, 7. 3–4, and 10 through 20 communicated by Mrs. John B. King, Williamston, 1913. Editorial emendations are indicated in parentheses. Reprinted by permission of the publishers from Reed Smith, *South Carolina Ballads*, pp. 125–28 (Cambridge, Mass.: Harvard University Press, 1928).

High and a high and a high holiday
Upon the very first of the year
Little Matthew Groves started out to the church
The holy word for to hear
The holy word for to hear

First passed him by a gay young bride
And the next passed him by was a pearl
And the third passed him by was Lord Donald's wife
The fairest of the three

Lord Donald's wife went out to town
To hear the Holy Word
Little footpage was standing near
A-listening what was said

He heard her ask Little Matty Grove(s)
To go home with her tonight
Come along with me Little Matthew she said
This night in my arms for to lie

O no oh no (oh no) he said
I dare not for my life
For I know by the gold rings on your fingers
That you are Lord Donald's wife

And what if I am Lord Donald's wife
Lord Donald is not at home
He's gone to the new academy
King Henry for to see

A little foot page was standing by
And he took to his heels and he run
He run he run to the broad riverside
And tuck to his belly and swum

He ran till he came to King Henry's gate
And tingled at the ring
And none so ready as Lord Donald himself
To get up and let him in

What news what news my little foot page
What news have you for me
Little Matthew Groves is at your own house
In bed with your gay lady

Lord Donald your wife went out of town today
To hear the Holy Word
And I heard her ask Little Matty Grove(s)
To bed with her tonight

If this is a lie you've told to me
I'll hang you to a tree
And if this is the truth you've told to me
My daughter your bride shall be

(What's this what's this cried Little Matty Groves
What's this so loud and shrill)
I hear Lord Donald's horn a-blowing
A-coming over the hill

Lie still lie still Little Matty Grove(s)
And go to sleep (said she)
It's nothing but papa's little shipping boys
A-driving the lambs to the ford

From that they fell to a chat of talk
From that to a doze of sleep
(At morning light) when they woke
Lord Donald was standing at the feet

It's how do you like my bed he says
And how do you like my sheet
And how do you like my gay lady
A-lying in your arms asleep

I like your bed very well Lord Donald
And I like your sheet
But I think more of your gay lady
A-lying in my arms asleep

Rise you up Little Matty Grove(s)
And draw on your fine suit
For I don't want it said when I am dead
That I slewed a naked man

And very the first lick was Little Matty Grove's
He caused the blood to run
The very next lick was Lord Donald's
He drove Little Matty Grove(s) to the floor

I think very well of you Lord Donald
I think very well of your kin
But I think heap more of Little Matty Grove(s)
Than I do of you and your kin

Oh don't you hear them little birds sing
Oh don't you hear them cry
Lord Donald has killed two people today
And tomorrow he must die die
And tomorrow he must die

EXAMPLE 15.
An Old Man Came Tumbling Home
(Child 274)

Communicated by P.W.C., C.H.C., W.J.K., Jr., and R.S., of Columbia, n.d. Reprinted by permission of the publishers from Reed Smith, *South Carolina Ballads*, pp. 159–61 (Cambridge, Mass.: Harvard University Press, 1928).

An old man came tumbling home
As drunk as he could be
He found a horse within the stall
Where his horse ought to be

My dear wife my kind wife
My loving wife says he
Whose horse is that within the stall
Where my horse ought to be

You poor fool you (blind) fool [sic]
You son of a (gun) says she [sic]
That's nothing but a milk-cow
Your mother gave to me

I've traveled the wide world over
I've sailed from shore to shore
But a saddle on a milk-cow
I never have seen before

EXAMPLE 16.
Mary on the Wild Moor
(Laws P 21)

This is a reconstruction of the version sung more than a generation ago by Paul Herbert Wesley of Murrells Inlet. Collected by C.W.J. from his daughters, Mae Wesley Morse, Jean Wesley Dusenbury, and June Wesley Elliott, 1966–67.

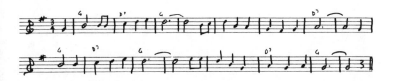

One night when the winds blew cold
Blew bitter across the wild moor
Young Mary came with her child
Wandering home to her own father's door

Oh father please let me in
Don't turn me away from your door
The child at my bosom will die
From the winds that blow across the wild moor

But the father was deaf to her cries
Not the sound of her voice passed the door
The watchdogs did bark but the winds
Grew bitter across the wild moor

Oh how must the father have felt
When he went to the door the next morn
There he found Mary dead and the child
Fondly clasped in its dead mother's arms

51

The child to the grave was soon borne
The father in grief passed away
The cottage to ruin has gone
And no one lives there to this day

The villagers point out the spot
Where a willow droops over the door
Where Mary perished and died
From the winds that blew across the wild moor

EXAMPLE 17.
The Drowsy Sleeper
(Laws M 4)

As sung by Eva Esdorn, Murrells Inlet, August 1969. Recorded by C.W.J.

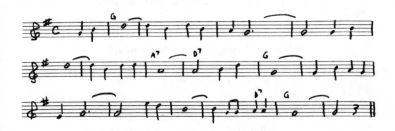

Who is at my bedroom window
Who is that this time of night
It is I your old true lover
Weeping under the willow tree

Mary Mary go and ask your mother
If she'll consent you to be my wife
If she says no come quickly and tell me
This night no longer I'll bother thee

It is no use to ask my mother
For she intends to keep me free
So Willie dear go and court some other
Another girl you'll love like me

I can court some other fair girl
I can climb the tallest trees
But Mary dear there's none I love
There's none I love as well as thee

Mary Mary go and ask your father
If he'll consent you to be my bride
If he says no come quickly and tell me
This night no longer I'll bother thee

It is no use to ask my father
For he intends to keep me free
So Willie dear please leave me forever
For there's none I love as well as thee

Willie pulled out his golden dagger
Stabbed it through his aching heart
Goodbye Mary goodbye darling
I am now at rest with thee

Mary picked up the golden dagger
Stabbed it through her milk-white breast
Goodbye Mama goodbye Daddy
I and Willie are now at rest

EXAMPLE 18.
Down with the Old Canoe
(Laws D 24)

Recorded by the Dixon Brothers (Dorsey and Howard) of Darlington in Charlotte, N.C., January 25, 1938. "Smoky Mountain Ballads," RCA Victor LPV-507. Transcribed by C.W.J.

It was twenty-five years ago when the wings of death came
    low
And spread out on the ocean far and wide
A great ship sailed away with her passengers so gay
To never never reach the other side

(Chorus:)

Sailing out to win her fame the *Titanic* was her name
When she had sailed five hundred miles from shore
Many passengers and her crew went down with that old
    canoe
They all went down to never ride no more

This great ship was built by men that is why she could not
    stand
She could not sink was the cry from one and all
But an iceburg ripped her side and it cut down all her pride
They found the hand of God was in it all

(Chorus)

Your *Titanic* sails today on life's breezes far away
But Jesus Christ can take you safely through
Just obey his great command over there you'll safely land
You'll never go down with that old canoe

(Chorus)

When you think that you are wise then you need not be
    surprised
If the hand of God should stop you on life's sea
If you go on in your sins you will find out in the end
That you are just as foolish as can be

(Chorus)

EXAMPLE 19.
Naomi Wise
(Laws F 31)

As sung by Minnie Floyd, Murrells Inlet, 1937. Recorded by
John A. Lomax. Library of Congress. Transcribed by C.W.J.

Come ye good people I pray you draw near.
A sorrowful story you shortly shall hear
A story I will tell you of Naomi Wise
And how she was deluded by Lewis's lies

When he first came to see me behaving so well
He promised to marry me and used me so well
Until they compar-ed to see if it was I
Oh how she was deluded by Lewis's lies

He promised to meet me at Adam's Spring
Some money to bring me or other fine things
Nothing he brought me but flattered the case
He said we'd get married and have no disgrace

He said if I'd go with him straightway to the town
Oh there we'd get married in union be bound
I jumped up behind him straightway we did go
To the banks of Deep River where the waters do flow

He said now Naomi I'll tell you my mind
I intend here to drown you and leave you behind
Oh pity me oh pity me and spare me my life
And I will go rejected and not be your wife

No mercy no mercy this monster did cry
In the bottom of Deep River your body shall lie

The vill-i-an did choke her as we do understand
And throwed her in Deep River below the mill dam
He jumped on his horse and he rode in great speed
He said now Naomi from you I'll be free

Behind sat poor Naomi still followed him so live
She says I'm a rebel that's not fit to die

Naomi was missing they all did well know
And hunting for her to the river did go
Her man found a clothes-pin on the water so deep
Which caused all the people to mourn and to weep

They lay birthmarks in for to see the great sight
How she lay a-floating all at low tide

EXAMPLE 20.
Delia Holmes
(Laws I 5)

The text and tune of the Will Winn version plus notes and
a fragmentary variant are published in Chapman J. Milling,
"Delia Holmes: A Neglected Negro Ballad," *Southern Folk-
lore Quarterly*, I (1937), 3–8. Dr. Milling's singing of
"Delia" was recorded for the Library of Congress by Charles
Seeger in Columbia, 1939. Used by permission of Chapman
J. Milling.

Delia, Delia, Why don't you run
See dat desparado had a forty fo' smokeless gun
Cryin' all I had done gone

(Chorus—repeated every six or eight stanzas)
All I had done gone All I had done gone
Good-bye Mother friends and all
All I had done gone

Now Coonie an his little sweetheart settin' down talkin' low
Axed her would she marry him she said why sho
Cryin' all I had done gone

When the time come for marriage she refuse' to go
If you don't marry me you cannot live no mo'
Cryin' all I had done gone

Shot her with a pistol number forty fo'
You did not marry me you cannot live no mo'
Cryin' all I had done gone

Turned po' Delia over on her side very slow
She was cryin' Coonie please don't shoot no mo'
Cryin' all I had done gone

Death had proceeded it wasn't so very long
Till her mother come runnin' with a bucket on her arm
Cryin' all I had done gone

Tell me my darlin' what have you done wrong
Cause Coonie to shoot you with that forty fo' smokeless gun
Cryin' all I had done gone

Some give a nickel some give a dime
Help to bury this body of mine
Cryin' all I had done gone

Threw down his pistol an' tried to get away
Officers picked him up in just a few days
Cryin' all I had done gone

Placed him in the jail till his trial should come
Tell me now officer what have I done
Cryin' all I had done gone

They axed him did he remember this a girl that you were
        in love
An' spoken things unto her that instantly taken her nerve
Cryin' all I had done gone

She moved closely beside of me an' threw her arms around
Do you remember little Delia Holmes and which you shot
        down
Cryin' all I had done gone

Have I now any bond or can I get one
For the crime that I am charged I plead guilty I have done
Cryin' all I had done gone

The judge that tried him handsome with the time
Say Coonie if I don't hang you
I'll give you ninety nine
Cryin' all I had done gone

Ninety nine years in prison workin' 'mont the stone
Hope that you'll get sorry that you have wrecked a home
Cryin' all I had done gone

Coonie went to Atlanta drinkin' from a silver cup
Po' li'l Delia's in the cemetery
I hope to never wake up
Cryin' all I had done gone

Delia's mother taken a trip out west
Just to keep from herin' the talk of po' li'l Delia's death
Cryin' all I had done gone

Everywhere the train would stop you could hear the people
    moan
Singin' dat lonesome song Po' Delia's dead an' gone
Cryin' all I had done gone

Rubber tire' buggy rubber tire' hack
Take you to de cemetary don't never bring you back
Cryin' all I had done gone

Coonie wrote to the Governor asked him pardon me
I was charged with murder in the first degree
Cryin' all I had done gone

The judge was liberal in givin' me my time
Happened that he didn't hang me but he gave me ninety
    nine
Cryin' all I had done gone

I am now a murderer serving a long, long time
And if you will pardon me I'll not be guilty of another
    crime
Cryin' all I had done gone

This is Coonie in Atlanta workin' 'mong the stone
Have been here for forty five years and I'm now needed at
    home
Cryin' all I had done gone

CHAPTER THREE

Religious Songs

Religious songs have been a cherished part of South Carolina's folk song heritage for three centuries. The religious songs of South Carolina run a gamut from the "shout" (or "ring-shout"), a survival of an African circle dance, to the religious ballad, which imposes sacred texts upon secular tunes such as those used for the British ballads "Barbara Allen" and "Lord Lovel." Perhaps the best-known and best-loved of all the religious folk songs of South Carolina, however, are the spirituals. The spirituals, or something very much like them, were sung in South Carolina as early as the Great Revival at the beginning of the nineteenth century. They show these early South Carolinians to be thoughtful and devout human beings, and reveal some of their aspirations to all who care to listen.

The eighteenth century witnessed a population explosion in South Carolina as in the other British colonies. While perhaps most of the early settlers migrated westward across the Blue Ridge and Great Smoky mountains, thousands of new settlers pushed down along the eastern slopes of these ranges and spread out into the piedmont. These pioneers—dissenters, poor, dispossessed, socially unacceptable—settled all over the Carolina upcountry, seeking a place where they could work their own land away from slavery and slaveholders. In the Old World they had been peasants or city slum-dwellers. In the New World they sought an opportunity to make a better living and to practice a more democratic faith. These nonconformists were delivered by the American Revolution not only from the control of the English government, but of the established church as well.

More numerous, perhaps, than any other group in the upcountry were the "Scotch-Irish," or "Ulster Scots"—Scots lowlanders who migrated to America after having been colonized in Northern Ireland. By 1775 the Scotch-Irish made up half the population of South Carolina. If we take into consideration the normally high rural birthrate of these folk, along with their hostility to the established church and slaveholders and their desire to escape from lowcountry control, it would seem likely that the preponderance of the upcountry settlers in the late eighteenth century were Scotch-Irish, although there were also English, Scots, Irish, Welsh, and German settlers.

The upcountry was swept by a wave of religious fervor during the Great Awakening before the American Revolution and during the Great Revival after the Revolution. The poor, the social outcasts, the blacks, all flocked to hear the new, more democratic gospel. Part of this religious fervor found expression in the new hymnody. With new denominations—Wesleyan Methodists and a variety of Baptists—came new or made-over hymns; and the most potent influence in the new hymn-making was that of the universally known and loved folk tunes of the people. Impressed on his American visit by the power of hymnody and with the need for songs to match the soaring emotions of the dissenting sects, John Wesley published his first hymns in Charleston in 1737. The new hymnody of John and Charles Wesley and of Isaac Watts resulted in hymns characterized by a new textual freedom. With more personal emotion and spiritual spontaniety the hymns were brought closer to the hearts of the people. Texts spoke directly of the woes and problems of the folk who sang them.

The South Carolina uncountry and the Southern colonies in general proved fertile ground for the further development of this trend in hymnody. To textual freedom the people added another element: they took the liberty of singing their hymns to tunes they already knew. In the upcountry unlettered folk sang the words of the new hymns to secular tunes passed on for generations in their families. Clothed in dignified—but not too dignified—religious texts, the tunes of such secular ballads as "Barbara Allen" and "Lord Lovel" were pressed into the service of the Lord. These ballads and other kinds of music which later generations would call folksongs had endured in the colony from the beginning, augmented by subsequent waves of British settlers. In bringing jigs, country dances, and old love songs and ballads into hymnody, these folk were not merely religious radicals, they were musical revolutionaries as well. This showed no lack of respect for religion; on the contrary, the upcountry folk brought one of their most loved and treasured possessions—their musical heritage—and laid it on the altar of their faith.

Sacred texts set to Celtic dance tunes may seem a strange combination. To many God-fearing folk, fiddles and all that went with them were the instruments of the devil. But those fiddle tunes were too catchy and insidious, too memorable, to remain Satan's exclusive possession for long. "Fisher's Hornpipe," a fiddle-bagpipe tune from the British Isles, served as the melody for a number of religious songs, among them "Legacy" (Example 21).

"Sawyer's Exit" (Example 22), pairs the tune of "Old Rosin the Bow" with a set of words said to have been composed on his deathbed by Rev. S. B. Sawyer who requested that they be fitted to this tune. The tune was widely known among the American folk. With appropriate words it even served as campaign songs for Henry Clay, Abraham Lincoln, and Ulysses S. Grant.

The introduction of folk tunes into hymnody produced a variety of types of religious folk tunes, ranging from the religious ballad, through the folk hymn to the spiritual. The religious ballads were songs for individual singing rather than for groups. In many of them the singer tells his story in the first person—such as the story of the poor wayfaring stranger, just a-going over Jordan, or of the dying or departing preacher or missionary. Saints as well as sinners would seem to have been fond of their swan songs. The text of "Hicks' Farewell" (Example 23) was penned by the Rev. Berryman Hicks (1778–1839), a Spartanburg, S.C., revivalist, who wrote it to his wife while ill of a fever in Tennessee and expecting that he would not recover.

By the beginning of the nineteenth century in the South the post-Wesleyan tide of religious revivalism was high. Hungry for entertainment and self-expression, the people flocked to hear shouting Baptist and Methodist evangelists call them to repentance and salvation, and preach hellfire and damnation to the rich, the rulers, the educated, and the privileged sinners. They gathered in huge encampments— still known in the rural South as camp meetings. There had been outdoor meetings before during the Great Awakening, but they took on new dimensions during the Great Revival. The upcountry camp meetings were marked by a soul-saving orgy of such emotional phenomena as fainting, swooning, jerking, barking, and shouting in tongues.

The camp meeting revivalists were no longer satisfied with the old and stately hymns of the more dignified denominations, and their musical debt to the dirge-like and dragged-out psalm tunes of pre-Revival colonial days was modest. The revivalists were willing to appropriate the melodic trends of the older songs insofar as they would fit and not become a hindrance to general participation. The revivalists' need, however, was less to induce the congregation to sing than to simplify the songs until they were an irresistible temptation to join in. The solution lay in progressively simplifying the text until a new song-type, the spiritual, had emerged. A fetching example of one of these simplified camp meeting songs is "Bringing in That New

Jerusalem" (Example 24). Its use of repeated lines and incremental verses made it very easy to learn.

To answer the needs of outdoor preaching and shouting congregations, these folk hymns often adopted the call-and-response pattern known as "lining out." The song leader would chant a line or two of the hymn, and the congregation would sing the same line after him. Harmony in the usual European sense was neglected in favor of part-singing which preferred interesting horizontal parts for each singer to vertical chords which combined all the voices. This liberation from harmony lent a melodic and rhythmic freedom to the music.

The slaves often attended white religious services in South Carolina, and they flocked to hear these Methodist and Baptist evangelists preach a gospel of equality before God. It is known that the blacks were especially fond of the camp meeting songs and blended their voices with whites in learning them and singing them. At the camp meetings, the blacks found themselves among those whites who harbored the least racial prejudice and whose religious practices came nearest their own African religious customs. Not only were the blacks allowed to attend the revivals and participate in the singing; they were invited to repentance, salvation, and full membership. Black people were converted in large numbers during the Great Revival. Many of these evangelists were interested not merely in the souls of black folk, but also with the release of their bodies from bondage.

While white men played the principal part in these camp meetings, black men were not merely passive spectators in the revivals, but participated fully. The behavior of white participants was decisively influenced by their black fellow-converts, even though the blacks brought greater rhythm and spontaniety to the revival compared with the more convulsive and jerky movements of the whites. While the forms of camp meeting behavior have generally been accepted as an outgrowth of the European inheritance, certain practices closely resembled African customs. Baptism by total immersion, for example, corresponded rather closely to customs of West African river cults, and the uninhibited manner of "getting religion" was very similar to West African spirit possession.

In the early nineteenth century unauthorized songbook publishers, catering to the new folk hymnody movement, brought out collections of texts of the camp meeting songs, without music. By the 1830s these songs, along with early psalm tunes, anthems, "fuguing songs," and religious ballads, were being compiled into "shape-note" hymnbooks, in which the pitch was indicated by the shape of the notes, independently of their position on the staff. The early camp meeting folk had rarely seen any notated form of their tunes, but the shape-note hymnbook makers—probably out of a desire to make their books more widely sought—incorporated more and more folk tunes of the camp meeting type as the years went by. Many of these songs are in the old modes and include the tunes of ballads, folk songs, country dances—and even Morris-dances.

The first rural shape-note hymnbook to attract wide attention was the product of a young South Carolinian who was born in the foothills of the Appalachians. William Walker was born May 6, 1809, near Cross Keys, Union County, but moved to the neighborhood of Cedar Spring in the Spartanburg district at the age of 18. After joining the Baptist church, he published in 1835 a shape-note hymnal entitled *The Southern Harmony*. To distinguish himself from others of the same name, he identified himself as William Walker, A.S.H. (author Southern Harmony). To thousands of people in the rural South, however, he was known as "Singing Billy." His hymnbook became so popular that it was sold in general stores along with groceries and tobacco, and its popularity continued to increase. By the outbreak of the Civil War more than half a million copies had been sold. Not content with the success of *The Southern Harmony*, Walker brought out an even more elaborate hymnal, which he prepared and published under the title *The Christian Harmony*. It was almost equally popular.

The Southern Harmony contained many tunes adopted from British balladry, including "Wondrous Love" (Example 25), to the tune of the old ballad of "Captain Kidd." Despite the British derivation of the tunes, Walker's settings, generally in three-part harmonies, imparted a distinctive American sound to the music.

Rivaling the *Southern Harmony* in popularity from the start, and far surpassing it in longevity, was *The Sacred Harp*, compiled by another South Carolinian, Benjamin Franklin White. White, who was born September 20, 1800, near Spartanburg, was Walker's brother-in-law and assisted him in putting together *The Southern Harmony*. After a disagreement in which White accused Walker of having unfairly changed the manuscript to deprive him of his rightful credit and of having conspired with Northern publishers to defraud him of his rightful interest in *The Southern Harmony*, White began work on his own shape-note hymnbook, *The Sacred Harp*, which he brought out in 1844. Unlike the other shape-note hymnals of the time, *The Sacred Harp* still remains in wide use in the rural South. The first edition of the *Sacred Harp* included the earliest known recording of "Wayfaring Stranger" (Example 26).

There was some difference in the notes as they looked on the printed page of such hymnals as *The Southern Harmony* and *The Sacred Harp* and as they sounded when actually sung. The singing tempi were more rapid; the singers got in more notes per minute. The singers disliked repeating the same note in long sequences for succeeding words or syllables in the text, and tended to substitute other notes as they felt like it. Still another difference was the penchant of the singers toward melodic decoration. Hymns made from Southern folk tunes usually displayed all these characteris-

tics; those from elsewhere were generally "Southernized"—
that is, they had these characteristics grafted on them.

This improvisatory process marked the development of
white religious music from the early nineteenth-century
revivals on. The inevitable movement was toward simplicity
of language, ascendance of feeling over meaning, repetition
of texts, and choruses coming every four lines or refrains
coming every line or two. In other words, the inevitable
movement was in the direction of leader-chorus form of
song—the most favored song-form of West Africa. Thus it
would seem that the Great Revival, with its camp meetings,
had made possible a subtle, but extensive blending of British
and West African music, and that black as well as white
Southerners had some hand in shaping the development of
Southern white hymnody away from its British models
toward a distinctive American style.

The first Negro spirituals to come to national attention
were collected on St. Helena Island by Charlotte L. Forten
and were published in the *Atlantic Monthly* in May 1864.
Later, Thomas Wentworth Higginson, a white northerner
who had commanded a black regiment in the state during
the Civil War, published some of his collection in the
Atlantic Monthly in June 1867. They were included with
the gleanings of other collectors in *Slave Songs of the
United States,* published later the same year. Of the 136
songs in the volume, 79 were from South Carolina, many of
them from St. Helena Island. The collectors were all white
Northerners who had first come into contact with black
Southerners during the war.

To understand the complexity of the spirituals and their
relation to the spiritual life of the slaves required an insight
lacking in many of the collectors. For one thing, they were
easily misled by the nearly incomprehensible Gullah dialect
of the lowcountry blacks. While the white collectors believed this dialect they scarcely understood was merely a
corruption of the English tongue, more recent scholarship
has revealed that the source of their confusion was deeper

than they thought. Comparative study of the Bantu and Sudanese dialects of West Africa with the Gullah of the Sea Islands revealed that Gullah remained relatively close to its African roots and retained thousands of African words.

The collectors found it especially difficult to describe the renditions of the songs which they compiled. William F. Allen, in his introduction to the *Slave Songs,* wrote: "The voices of the colored people have a peculiar quality that nothing can imitate; and the intonations and delicate variations of even one singer cannot be reproduced on paper. And I despair of conveying any notion of the effect of a number singing together."

Allen and Ware were much taken with the black Carolinians' "exquisite time." They "do not suffer themselves to be daunted by any obstacle in the words," the editors wrote, "and will dash heroically through a trochaic tune at the head of a column of iambs with wonderful skill."

Many of the Northern visitors received their first introduction to the spirituals while being rowed across Port Royal Sound from Beaufort to St. Helena Island. Charlotte Forten, an educated and idealistic Northern Negro who had come to teach the freedmen on St. Helena, described the experience in her journal: "It was just at sunset—a grand Southern sunset; and the gorgeous clouds of crimson and gold were reflected in the waters below, which were smooth and calm as a mirror. Then, as we glided along, the rich sonorous tones of the boatmen broke upon the evening stillness. Their singing impressed me much. It was so sweet and strange and solemn. . . ."

> Jesus make da blind to see
> Jesus make de deaf to hear
> Jesus make de cripple walk
> Walk in dear Jesus

The rowing crews sang two measures to each stroke of the oars. The first measure was accented by the beginning of

the stroke, the second by the rattle of the oars in the oar-
locks as they returned to begin another stroke. The crews on
the passenger boats at the Beaufort ferry rowed an average
of 24 strokes per minute—anywhere from 16 to 30 strokes
per minute, depending on the wind and tide. A favorite rowing song of the crews when the load was heavy or when they
had to row against the tide was "Michael Row the Boat
Ashore" (Example 27).

To Northern visitors, the primitive "shouting" spirituals,
developed by black Southerners more or less independently
of the white camp meetings, were the most striking mani-
festations of the African spirit. Charlotte Forten considered
them "wild and strange." She had much difficulty understanding the words, even though she asked the singers to
repeat them for her. The shouts seemed "barbarous" to her.
They had been "handed down," she believed, from the
slaves' "African ancestors, and [were] destined to pass away
under the influence of Christian teachings."

Despite her initial distaste for the shouts, or "ring-shouts,"
Charlotte Forten was correct in attributing their origin to
Africa. The shout pattern is demonstrably West African in
origin, a circle dance which survived, more or less by acci-
dent, almost intact. Taking their newly acquired Christianity
back to the slave quarters, the black Carolinians worshipped
their new Christian God in their own fashion, by singing,
dancing, and spirit-possession. The drum rhythms which had
figured in their West African religious ceremonies were
easily improvised by clapping and stomping. The main difference was that the words were now in English. The slaves
called this phenomenon a *Saut,* or shout, using a word current in West Africa meaning to walk or run around.
Sometimes a shout was a feature of conversion.

James Weldon Johnson has noted that the shouts were
often "looked down upon by a great many colored people.
. . . These songs are not true spirituals nor even truly religious. . . . They might be termed quasi-religious-savage
music." The Sea Islanders, however, drew a distinction be-

tween dancing and shouting. "Dancing in the usual way is
regarded with great horror by the people of Port Royal,"
wrote Allen, "but they enter with infinite zest into the movements of the 'shout'." According to Laura M. Towne, the
founder of the freedmen's school on St. Helena Island, however much dancing "out in de world" might be disapproved,
it was perfectly permissible for the church members to
"strive behind the Elders."

There are a number of interesting descriptions of shouts
from people who have seen them. Colonel Thomas Wentworth Higginson, commander of the First South Carolina
Volunteers, the first slave regiment mustered into the service
of the United States during the Civil War, wrote in his
Army Life in a Black Regiment: "Often in the starlit evening I have returned from some lonely ride by the swift
river, or on the plover-haunted barrens, and, entering the
camp, have silently approached some glimmering fire, round
which the dusky figures moved in the rhythmical barbaric
dance the negroes call a 'shout,' chanting, often harshly, but
always in the most perfect time, some monotonous refrain."
The songs, Higginson reported, were sung with no accompaniment save the clapping of hands and the stomping of
feet. The most popular song in camp was "Hold Your Light,
Brudder Robert" (Example 28). He dubbed another popular and picturesque shout the "Romandar" (Example 29).

Charlotte Forten gradually came under the spell of the
shouts, eventually even pronouncing them "grand" and "inspiring." "There is an old blind man, Maurice," she wrote
in her journal, "Who has a truly wonderful voice, so strong
and clear.—It rings out like a trumpet. One song—"Gabriel
Blow the Trumpet"—was the grandest thing I have yet
heard. And with what fire and enthusiasm the old blind
man led off. He seemed inspired."

A few days later she heard him sing again: "Old Maurice
surpassed himself tonight in singing 'The Talles' Tree in
Paradise.' He got much excited and his gestures were really
quite tragic." Almost certainly the song to which she re-

ferred was "Blow Your Trumpet, Gabriel," collected by Ware in the Sea Islands and included in the *Slave Songs* (Example 30).

The shout is still to be found in the Sea Islands of South Carolina. Guy Carawan, a young white man who came to Johns Island as part of Highlander Folk School's extension program of adult education, attended a traditional Christmas Eve all-night watch at Moving Star Hall in 1959. In his report, he wrote:

A woman with a thick rich low alto started off in the corner and very soon was joined by some deep resonant male "basers" from another corner. Then falsetto wails and moans sailed in to float on high over the lead. By the time the whole group of about sixty worshippers had joined in, each freely improvising in his own way, the hall was rocking and swaying. . . . All sorts of overlapping parts and complementary sounds wove and blended together to produce a breathtaking whole full of rough beauty. I've never heard such colors in the human voice before. Some people did things with their voices that I don't think anyone could duplicate unless he'd grown up in that tradition....

From the moment the watch started with the first song, heads and bodies began to sway, feet to tap, and hands to clap in time to the singing. They sang with their whole bodies. These motions increased in abandonment as the evening went along until finally the "shouting" started. Someone stood and started rocking back and forth doing a special rhythmic step and hand clap in time to the singing. Others followed, and by the end of the song the whole group was on its feet singing, dancing, and clapping a joyous noise to the Lord. The whole building was rocking in time. Three different rhythms were being carried by the hands, feet, and voice.

One of the favorite shouts on Johns Island is "Been in the Storm So Long" (Example 31).

The inspirational genesis of the spirituals, according to James Weldon Johnson, was the fusion of African musical instincts with the spirit of Christianity. "The result was a body of songs voicing all the cardinal virtues of Christianity —patience, forbearance, love, faith, and hope in a more glorious future life for those who suffered most here, through a modified form of primitive African music." Had the slaves not adopted Christianity, he was certain there would have been no spirituals. Indeed, he doubted if the slaves, without Christianity, would have been able to survive their bondage in the manner in which they did. "How much this firm faith had to do with the Negro spiritual and physical survival of slavery cannot be known." Christianity, Johnson felt, was the "precise religion" for the lot of the slave: "The religion of meekness, of submission, of contentment with the ills of this existence — the religion of compensations in the life to come for the ills suffered in present existence — a religion that implied the hope that in the next world there would be a reversal of conditions of rich men and poor, of master and slave."

Colonel Higginson noted the same attitude of patience in this life, triumph in the next, in the spirituals. "The attitude is always, and, as a commentary on the life of the race, is infinitely pathetic." Man's infinite longing for peace from suffering, he believed, was never more plaintively expressed than in the spiritual "Lay Dis Body Down" (Example 32).

Peace from suffering is not the only peace longed for in the South Carolina spirituals. There is no more pacifistic song than the South Carolina version of "Study War No More" (Example 33).

Ellen Murray, an associate of Laura Towne in the St. Helena school, believed the "true religion" had wrought a significant effect upon the religion of the freedmen of the island. "The fear of death," she noted, "seems to be in a great measure obliterated by their own numerous songs of heaven." One who could sing such songs as "Stars Begin to Fall" (Example 34) was not likely to fear the reality of death.

Not all the spirituals exemplified meekness or submission. Colonel Higginson recognized a quality of stoic courage implicit in the spirituals. To the black soldiers of the First South Carolina Volunteers they were "more than a source of relaxation; they were a stimulus to courage and a tie to heaven." One of the South Carolina spirituals which expresses this quality of stoic courage with great force is "Road Is Rugged, But I Must Go" (Example 35).

Some of the songs collected by Colonel Higginson played historic roles during the Civil War. Slaves in Georgetown, for example, were jailed early in the war for singing "We'll Soon Be Free" (Example 36). The song was not new, though it was probably chanted with renewed vigor when war broke out.

The white men's suspicions in the case of "We'll Soon Be Free" were unfounded, or mostly so; but there were topical songs which commented directly on the war and imminent emancipation. "Many Thousand Gone" (Example 37) was one such song. Higginson wrote of it: "This was composed by nobody knew whom — though it was the most recent, doubtless, of all these 'spirituals,'—and had been sung in secret to avoid detection. It is certainly plaintive enough. The peck of corn and pint of salt were slavery's rations."

Thus, out of the musical traditions of West Africa and of the British Isles two important spiritual singing traditions developed in the South, each to some extent influenced by the other. The blending of cultures in the camp meetings was not a one-sided affair. The black spirituals are in no sense mere "borrowings" from white spirituals, nor are they purely or even mainly African. Few of the South Carolina spirituals fail to reveal at least some influence of Anglo-American folk music, but few indeed are lacking in the essential characteristics of the African tradition. Like so much else in Southern life, the black and white spirituals are the offspring of the mating of African and British folk cultures. This cultural integration was made possible by a unique coincidence of circumstances that did not occur elsewhere. Only in the South was a genuinely biracial folk culture created. The inheritance from West Africa and the inheritance from the British Isles were both essential to the creation of the new biracial folk culture; and South Carolina was fortunate enough to play a central role in its development.

EXAMPLE 21.
Legacy

From *Southern Harmony, and Musical Companion* (Philadelphia, 1854), p. 73.

When in death I shall calm recline
O bear my heart to my mistress dear
Tell her it lived upon smiles and wine
Of the brightest hue while it linger'd here

Bid her not shed one tear of sorrow
To sully a heart so brilliant and light
But balmy drops of the red grape borrow
To bathe the relic from morn to night

EXAMPLE 22.
Sawyer's Exit

From the 1859 edition of *The Sacred Harp*.

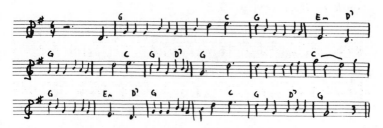

How bright is the day when the Christian
Receives the sweet message to come
To rise to the mansions of glory
And be forever at home

(Chorus)
And be there forever at home
And be there forever at home
To rise to the mansions of glory
And be there forever at home

The angels stand ready and waiting
The moment the spirit is gone
To carry it upward to heaven
And welcome it safely at home

The saints that have gone up before us
All raise a new shout as we come
And sing hallelujah the louder
To welcome the travelers home

77

EXAMPLE 23.
Hicks' Farewell

Words by Rev. Berryman Hicks. Music by William Walker.
Southern Harmony, p. 19.

The time is swiftly rolling on
When I must faint and die
My body to the dust return
And there forgotten lie

Let persecution rage around
And Antichrist appear
My silent dust beneath the ground
There's no disturbance there

My little children near my heart
And nature seems to bind
It grieves me sorely to depart
And leave you all behind

My loving wife my bosom friend
The object of my love
The time's been sweet I've spent with you
My sweet and harmless dove

My loving wife don't grieve for me
Neither lament nor mourn
For I shall with my Jesus be
When you are left alone

EXAMPLE 24.
Bringing in That New Jerusalem

As sung by Mrs. Genevieve Wilcox Chandler, Murrells
Inlet, August 1969. Collected by C.W.J.

I've got a mother who's gone to glory
I've got a mother who's gone to glory
I've got a mother who's gone to glory
Bringing in that new Je-ru-sa-LEM

(Chorus)
It's all free grace and never-dying love
It's all free grace and never-dying love
It's all free grace and never-dying love
Bringing in that new Je-ru-sa-LEM

I've got a father (brother, sister)
    who's gone to glory (3 times)
Bringing in that new Je-ru-sa-LEM

79

EXAMPLE 25.
Wondrous Love

The Southern Harmony, p. 252.

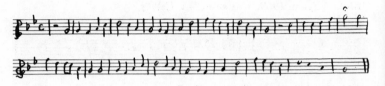

What wondrous love is this oh my soul oh my soul
What wondrous love is this oh my soul
What wondrous love is this that caused the Lord of bliss
To bear the dreadful curse for my soul

EXAMPLE 26.
Wayfaring Stranger

The Sacred Harp, 1844. Quoted in *Spiritual Folk Songs of Early America* (New York, 1937), pp. 70–71. Verses 1 and 2.

I am a poor wayfaring stranger
While trav'ling through this world of woe
Yet there's no sickness, toil nor danger
In that bright world to which I go
I'm going there to see my father
I'm going there no more to roam
I'm only going over Jordan I'm only going over home

I know dark clouds will gather round me
I know my way is rough and steep
Yet beauteous fields lie just before me
Where God's redeem'd their vigils keep
I'm going there to see my mother
She said she'd meet me when I come
I'm only going over Jordan
I'm only going over home.

EXAMPLE 27.
Michael Row the Boat Ashore

From Port Royal Island. Collected by Charles P. Ware. *Slave Songs of the United States* (New York, 1867), pp. 23–24.

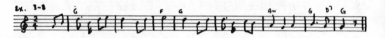

Michael row de boat ashore
Halelujah
Michael row de boat ashore
Halelujah

Michael boat a gospel boat (etc.)

I wonder where my mudder deh

See my mudder on de rock gwine home

On de rock gwine home in Jesus name

Michael boat a music boat

Gabriel blow de trumpet horn

O you mind your boastin talk

Boastin' talk will sink your soul

Brudder lend a helpin hand

Sister help for trim dat boat

Jordan stream is wide and deep

Jesus stand on t'oder side

I wonder if my maussa deh

My fader gone to unknown land

O de Lord he plant his garden deh

He raise de fruit for you to eat

He dat eat shall neber die

When de river overflow

O poor sinner how you land

Riber run and darkness comin'

Sinner row to save your soul

EXAMPLE 28.
Hold Your Light

As sung in the First South Carolina Volunteers. Collected by Thomas Wentworth Higginson. In Higginson, p. 199. See also *Slave Sings*, p. 10.

Hold your light Brudder Robert
Hold your light
Hold your light on Canaan's Shore

What make ole Satan for follow me so
Satan ain't got notin' for do wid me

Hold your light
Hold your light
Hold your light on Canaan's shore

EXAMPLE 29.
Room in Dar

As sung in the First South Carolina Volunteers. Collected by Thomas Wentworth Higginson. In Higginson, p. 200.

O my mudder is gone my mudder is gone
My mudder is gone into heaven my Lord
I can't stay behind

Dere's room in dar room in dar
Room in dar in de heaven my Lord
I can't stay behind

O my fader is gone (etc.)

O de angels are gone (etc.)

O I'se been on de road (etc.)

EXAMPLE 30.
Blow Your Trumpet, Gabriel

From Port Royal Island. Collected by Charles P. Ware. *Slave Songs*, p. 3.

De talles' tree in Paradise
De Christian call de tree of life
And I hope dat trump might blow me home
To de new Jerusalem

Blow your trumpet Gabriel
Blow louder louder
And I hope dat trump might blow me home
To de new Jerusalem

Paul and Silas bound in jail
Sing God's praise both night and day
And I hope dat trump might blow me home
To de new Jerusalem

EXAMPLE 31.

Been in the Storm So Long

As sung by Mrs. Mary Pinckney, Johns Island. Collected by Guy Carawan. In *Ain't You Got a Right to the Tree of Life? The People of Johns Island, South Carolina—Their Faces, Their Words and Their Songs*, recorded by Guy and Candie Carawan (New York, 1966), p. 51. Used by permission of Mrs. Janey Hunter for the Moving Star Hall Class Meeting.

I've been in the storm so long
You know I've been in the storm so long
Singin' Oh Lord give me more time to pray
I've been in the storm so long

I am a motherless child
Singin' I am a motherless child
Singin' Oh Lord give me more time to pray
I've been in the storm so long

This is a needy time
This is a needy time
Singin' Oh Lord give me more time to pray
I've been in the storm so long

Lord I need you now (etc.)

Lord, I need your prayer (etc.)

Stop this wicked race (etc.)

Stop all my wicked ways (etc.)

Somebody need you now (etc.)

My neighbors need you now (etc.)

My children need you now (etc.)

Just look what a shape I'm in (etc.)

EXAMPLE 32.
Lay Dis Body Down

As sung in the First South Carolina Volunteers. Collected by Thomas Wentworth Higginson. In Higginson, pp. 208–209. See also *Slave Songs*, p. 19.

I know moon-rise I know star-rise
Lay dis body down

I walk in de moonlight I walk in de starlight
Lay dis body down

I'll walk in de graveyard I'll walk through de graveyard
Lay dis body down

I'll lie in de grave and stretch out my arms
Lay dis body down

I'll lie in de grave and stretch out my arms
Lay dis body down

I go to de judgment in de evenin' of de day
Lay dis body down

And my soul and your soul will meet in de day
Lay dis body down

EXAMPLE 33.
Going to Pull My War-Clothes

As sung at Frogmore, St. Helena Island, 1913. Collected by
Carl Diton. In *Thirty-Six South Carolina Spirituals,* ed.
Carl Diton (New York, 1928), pp. 24–25. Used by permission of G. Schirmer, Inc.

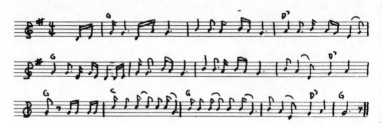

Going to pull my war-clothes
Down by the riverside
Down by the riverside
Down by the riverside
Going to pull my war-clothes
Down by the riverside
Study war no more

(chorus)
Yes I'm going to study war no more
Study war no more
Study war no more

Going to meet my brethren (etc.)

Going to meet my sister (etc.)

EXAMPLE 34.
Stars Begin to Fall

Probably from Edisto Island. Collected by Charles P. Ware.
In *Slave Songs*, pp. 25–26.

I tink I hear my brudder say
Call de nation great and small
I lookee on de God's right hand
When de stars begin to fall

Oh what a mournin' (sister)
Oh what a mournin' (brudder)
Oh what a mournin'
When de stars begin to fall

EXAMPLE 35.
Road Is Rugged, but I Must Go

As sung at Frogmore, St. Helena Island, 1913. Collected by Carl Diton. In Diton, pp. 32–35. Used by permission of G. Schirmer, Inc.

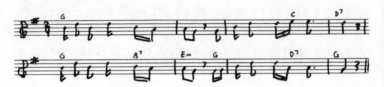

Road is rugged but I must go
I must go to see my Lord
Road is rugged but I must go
I must go to see my Lord

It's a field of battle but I must go
I must go to see my Lord
It's a field of battle but I must go
I must go to see my Lord

Road is rugged but I must go (etc.)

Got to pray so hard but I must go (etc.)

Road is rugged but I must go (etc.)

Jesus died and I must go (etc.)

Road is rugged but I must go (etc.)

EXAMPLE 36.
We'll Soon Be Free

Collected by Thomas Wentworth Higginson as sung by the
First South Carolina Volunteers. In Higginson, p. 217.

We'll soon be free
We'll soon be free
We'll soon be free
When de Lord will call us home

My brudder how long
My brudder how long
My brudder how long
'Fore we done sufferin' here

It won't be long
It won't be long
It won't be long
'Fore de Lord will call us home

We'll walk de miry road (3 times)
Where pleasure never dies

We'll walk de golden street (3 times)
Where pleasure never dies

My brudder how long (3 times)
'Fore we done sufferin' here

We'll soon be free (3 times)
When de Lord will call us home

We'll soon be free (3 times)
When Jesus sets me free

We'll fight for liberty (3 times)
When de Lord will call us home

EXAMPLE 37.
Many Thousand Gone

This song was first sung by the Sea Island slaves when
General P. G. T. Beauregard used them to build fortifica-
tions at Hilton Head and Bay Point. As sung in First South
Carolina Volunteers. Collected by Thomas Wentworth Higginson. In Higginson, p. 218, and *Slave Songs*, p. 48.

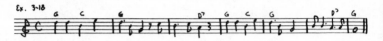

No more peck of corn for me
No more no more
No more peck o corn for me
Many tousand go

No more driver's lash for me
No more no more
No more driver's lash for me
Many tousand go

No more pint o salt for me (etc.)

No more hundred lash for me (etc.)

No more mistress' call for me (etc.)

CHAPTER FOUR

The Seculars

The West African folk inheritance had a stronger influence on white South Carolinians than has been generally understood. Many of them, remote from places where professional entertainment was presented, had as their only continuing form of entertainment the music and dances of their black neighbors. The interchange of styles and songs proceeded at an even greater pace with the secular songs than with the spirituals.

The interchange was facilitated by a widespread substitute among the whites for dancing to instrumental music. Because of the lack of musical instruments, or hostility to them, a song-dance form called the play-party was developed, which called for rhythmic dance steps to the accompaniment of rhythmically chanted words, a form similar to, and undoubtedly influenced by, West African dancing practices. Such play-party songs as "Shoe-Lie-Low" (Example 38) were chanted and danced to by both races.

Perhaps even more important in song-swapping across the color lines were the lullabies. Here the direction of the exchange seems to be primarily from black to white, probably because of the large number of white children who were raised by black women. One such lullaby, "All the Pretty Little Horses" (Example 39), originally a black creation, has become so widespread as to be regarded as common property of both races.

Perhaps the most influential form of black secular music on the music of white South Carolinians was the blues. They sing of tragedy and despair, and of hope and determination. Implicit in the blues is the whole history of black people in this country. The blues are seldom far away, always ready to trap the unwary, to take possession of the whole being, invincible, inescapable (Example 40).

The spread of the blues across the South in the early years of the twentieth century gave rise to all sorts of new forms in music—ragtime and jazz on the one hand, and hillbilly and country-and-western on the other. South Carolina had an important role to play in the development of jazz, culminating, perhaps, in the fabulous career of John Birks "Dizzy" Gillespie, a native of Cheraw. A South Carolinian who linked the worlds of jazz and folk music was the outstanding guitarist and singer Josh White, who was born in Greenville. The state's part in the development of country music is perhaps more easily recognized in the titles of important songs in the evolution of country music than in the names of their composers, but both Dorsey Dixon of Darlington, composer of "Wreck on the Highway," and Jimmie Tarleton of Chesterfield County, composer of "Columbus Stockade Blues," had important careers as country music performers in the 1920s and 1930s. Banjoist "Snuffy" Jenkins of Columbia played a seminal role in the creation of bluegrass music. Arthur "Guitar Boogie" Smith of Chester, China Poplin of Sumter, and Linda Martel of Columbia are currently popular country music personalities. Miss Martel, who has performed on Nashville's Grand Ole Opry, is the first black woman ever to achieve fame as a country-and-western singer.

Hillbilly music, and subsequently country-and-western, would not have developed without the essential influence of the blues in transforming the Anglo-American folk tradition. The Afro-American blues took an important place in the artistic and expressive life of white South Carolina musicians.

Between 1927 and the early 1940s, Jimmie Tarleton, son of a Chesterfield County cotton farmer, was a major figure in country music. One of the first, if not *the* first, hillbilly artists to use the steel guitar, Tarleton always sought an exciting sound in his music. In November 1927, he recorded two of his own compositions, "Columbus Stockade Blues" and "Birmingham Jail" for Columbia records. Their success propelled him to a distinguished career during the "golden age" of country music. It is significant that this pioneer hillbilly recording was a blues (Example 41).

In 1931, Tarleton met Dorsey Dixon, son of a Darlington textile worker, and began an association which was mutually inspiring. Dorsey and his brother Howard, as the Dixon Brothers, began a recording career with the Victor recording company. Between 1936 and 1938, the Dixon Brothers recorded some sixty songs for Victor, the most popular of which was easily Dorsey's composition, "Wreck on the Highway." More revealing, perhaps, was his use of the Afro-American musical form to describe life in the Southern mill villages, as in "Weave Room Blues" (Example 42).

An interesting mutation of the blues—the "talking blues" —was developed by another white South Carolinian, Chris Bouchillon. According to one story, the recording executive liked the way Bouchillon talked but not the way he sang, so he made Bouchillon recite to a rhythmic guitar backing, but without any definite rhyming or verse pattern. The result was "Born in Hard Luck" (Example 43). It wasn't long before Bouchillon had developed his mutation into a full-fledged new musical form, with four chanted lines, four beats to the line, and an A A B B rhyme scheme, followed by a couple of unrhymed comments. The harmonic form of the instrumental backing was firmly rooted in the blues, and the verses clearly suggest the Afro-American origins of the "Talking Blues" (Example 44).

Perhaps the classic case of musical integration is the case of "We Shall Overcome" (Example 45), which began its life as a hymn published in a white Baptist hymnbook.

Its authorship was attributed to the Reverend C. A. Tinsley. In the process of oral transmission, however, the verse tended to be forgotten, and attention focused on the chorus:

> I'll overcome some day
> I'll overcome some day
> If in my heart I do not yield
> I'll overcome some day.

Out among the folk, especially among black South Carolinians, the chorus became transformed over the decades. By 1946, when some black members of a food and tobacco workers' union in Charleston carried it to Highlander Folk School in Tennessee, the "I" had become "We" and more verses were added. Except for the substitution of "shall" for "will" and the addition of some specific verses during the Civil Rights movement of the early 1960s, the song had for all practical purposes assumed its present form by 1946 in South Carolina. Thus the folk-music interchange between the Anglo-American tradition and the Afro-American tradition continues in South Carolina. I believe this process has been a beneficial one for both races. In fact, I believe the extraordinary richness of South Carolina folk music is a direct result of this musical integration. Through this musical integration, our black and white ancestors have been in the process of creating a biracial folk culture for three hundred years.

EXAMPLE 38.
Shoe-Lie-Low

As sung by Mrs. Bob Watts, Murrells Inlet, August 1969.
Collected by C.W.J.

Stole my partner shoe lie low
Stole my partner shoe lie low
Stole my partner shoe lie low
Shoe lie low my darling

I'll get another shoe lie low
I'll get another shoe lie low
I'll get another shoe lie low
Shoe lie low my darling

Prettier than the other shoe lie low
Prettier than the other shoe lie low
Prettier than the other shoe lie low
Shoe lie low my darling

EXAMPLE 39.
All the Pretty Little Horses

As sung by Mrs. Bob Watts, Murrells Inlet, August 1969.
Collected by C.W.J.

Hey little black sheep where's your lamb
Way down yonder in the alley
Buzzards and the butterflies pickin' out its eyes
And the poor little thing cried Mammy

Go to sleep go to sleep
Go to sleep my baby
When you awake you shall have a cake
And all the pretty little horses

EXAMPLE 40.
Every Day of the Week

As sung by Pink Anderson, South Carolina street singer,
May 29, 1950. Riverside RLP 12-611.

I hate to leave you Mama God knows I sure hate to go
I hate to leave you Mama God knows I sure hate to go
Had the blues so long it made my poor heart so'

The blues jumped the devil run the devil a solid mile
The blues jumped the devil run the devil a solid mile
Well the devil set down and he cried like a new-born chile

EXAMPLE 41.
Columbus Stockade Blues

As sung by Jimmie Tarleton. Recorded November 10, 1927, Atlanta, Ga. Columbia 15212.

Way down in Columbus Georgia
Wanna be back in Tennessee
Way down in Columbus stockade
Friends have turned their backs on me

(Chorus)
Go and leave me if you wish to
Never let me cross your mind
In your heart you love some other
Leave me darling I don't mind

Many a night with you I've rambled
Many an hour I've been with you
Thought I gained your heart forever
Saw you have proved false to me

(Chorus)
Last night while I lay sleeping
I dreamed that I was in your arms
When I woke I was mistaken
I was peeping through the bars

EXAMPLE 42.
Weave Room Blues

As recorded by Dorsey and Howard Dixon. Bluebird 6441.
Copyright 1935 by Dorsey Dixon and Wade Mainer.

Working in a weave-room fighting for my life
Trying to make a living for my kiddies and my wife
Some are needing clothing and some are needing shoes
But I'm getting nothing but them weave-room blues

(Chorus)
I got the blues I got the blues
I got them awful weave-room blues
I got the blues the weave-room blues

With your looms a-slamming shuttles bouncing on the floor
And when you flag your fixer you can see that he is sore
I'm trying to make a living but I'm thinking I will lose
But I'm a-getting nothing but them weave room blues

(Chorus)
The harness eyes are breaking and the doubles coming
   through
The devil's in your alley and he's coming after you

103

Our hearts are aching let us take a little booze
For we're simply dying with them weave-room blues

(Chorus)
Slam outs break outs knot ups by the score
Cloth all rolled back and piled up in the floor
The bats are running ends and the strings are hanging to
   your shoes
We're simply dying with them weave-room blues

(Chorus)

EXAMPLE 43.
Born in Hard Luck

As recorded by Chris Bouchillon, Columbia 15151.

Now people I'm gonna tell you what a hard luck man I
    really am
Ya know I was born in hard luck
I was born in the last month in the year
The last week in the month
The last day in the week
The last hour in the day
The last minute in the hour
The last second in the minute
To tell the truth now I like not to have got here at all
Oh I'm hard luck all right

Ya know I was born down there in the country
On a little farm
Where the land's so poor that you got to put fertilizer
    around the telephone poles
Before you can talk over the wires
But its a good place to be from anyway

EXAMPLE 44.
Original Talking Blues

As recorded by Chris Bouchillon, c. 1927–28. In "The Art of
the Talking Blues," *Sing Out*, XV (January, 1966), 53–59.

Ain't no use me workin' so hard
I got a gal in the white folk's yard
When she kills a chicken she saves me the head
She thinks I'm working but I'm lyin' in bed
Sleepin'
Havin' a good time
Dreamin' about her

If you want to get to heaven let me tell you how to do it
Grease your feet with a little mutton suet
Slide right out of the devil's hand
And ooze right over in the Promised Land
Go easy
Make it easy
Go Greasy

Standin' on the corner standin' like a man
Standin' on the corner with a bucket in my hand
Standin' on the corner with a bucket in my hand
Waitin' for sop from the white folk's hand
'Lasses
Sweetlin' potatoes
Cold biscuits

EXAMPLE 45.
We Will Overcome

As sung by black South Carolinians at Highlander Folk
School, Monteagle, Tenn., 1945. Ms. in Zilphia Horton Folk
Music Collection, Tennessee State Library and Archives,
Nashville. Used by permission of Highlander Center.

We will overcome
We will overcome
We will overcome some day
Oh down in my heart
I do believe
We'll overcome some day

The Lord will see us through
The Lord will see us through
The Lord will see us through some day
Oh down in my heart
I do believe
We'll overcome some day

We're on to victory
We're on to victory
We're on to victory some day
Oh down in my heart

I do believe
We'll overcome some day

We will overcome
We will overcome
We will overcome some day
Oh down in my heart
I do believe
We'll overcome some day

Selected
Bibliography

Unpublished Materials

W. E. B. DuBois Papers, Yale University.

Highlander Folk School Manuscript Records Collection, Tennessee State Library and Archives, Nashville.

Zilphia Horton Folk Music Collection, Tennessee State Library and Archives, Nashville.

Arthur Palmer Hudson Folklore Collection, University of North Carolina, Chapel Hill.

James Weldon Johnson Papers, Yale University.

John A. Lomax Folk Song Collection, Folk Song Archive, Library of Congress.

Books

Allen, William F., Ware, Charles P., and Garrison, Lucy M. *Slave Songs of the United States* (New York: 1867).

Abrahams, Roger, and Foss, George. *Anglo-American Folksong Style* (Englewood Cliffs, N. J.: 1968).

Ballanta, N. G. J. *Saint Helena Island Spirituals* (New York: 1925).

Botkin, B. A. *A Treasury of Southern Folklore* (New York: 1949).

Brooks, Cleanth, Jr. *The Relation of the Alabama-Georgia Dialect to the Provincial Dialects of Great Britain* (Baton Rouge: 1935).

Carawan, Guy and Candie. *Ain't You Got a Right to the Tree of Life?* (New York: 1966).

Child, Francis James. *The English and Scottish Popular Ballads* (5 vols., Boston: 1882–1898).

Dorson, Richard M. *American Folklore* (Chicago: 1959).

Forten, Charlotte L. (Ed. Billington, Ray Allen) *The Journal of Charlotte L. Forten* (New York: 1953).

Gonzales, Ambrose E. *The Black Border* (Columbia: 1923).

Higginson, Thomas Wentworth. *Army Life in a Black Regiment* (New York: 1870).

Johnson, Guy B. *Folk Culture on St. Helena Island, South Carolina* (Chapel Hill: 1930).

Johnson, Guion Griffis. *A Social History of the Sea Islands* (Chapel Hill: 1930).

Laws, G. Malcolm, Jr. *American Balladry from British Broadsides* (Philadelphia: 1957).

———. *Native American Balladry* (Philadelphia: 1964).

Lomax, John A. *Adventures of a Ballad Hunter* (New York: 1947).

Rose, Willie Lee. *Rehearsal for Reconstruction* (Indianapolis: 1964).

Scarborough, Dorothy. *On the Trail of Negro Folk Songs* (Cambridge, Mass.: 1925).

———. *A Song Catcher in the Southern Mountains* (New York: 1937).

Smith, Reed. *South Carolina Ballads* (Cambridge, Mass.: 1928).

Stoney, Samuel G., and Shelby, Gertrude M. *Black Genesis: A Chronicle* (New York: 1930).

Towne, Laura M. (Ed. Holland, R. S.) *Letters and Diary of Laura M. Towne* (Cambridge, Mass.: 1912).

Turner, Lorenzo Dow. *Africanisms in the Gullah Dialect* (Chicago: 1949).

Walker, William. *Southern Harmony* (New Haven, Conn.: 1835).

White, Benjamin Franklin. *Sacred Harp* (Philadelphia: 1844).

White, N. I., Baum, Paull F., et al., Eds. *Frank C. Brown Collection of North Carolina Folklore* (6 vols., Durham, N. C.: 1952–1965).

Articles and Essays

Bascom, William R. "Acculturation Among the Gullah Negroes." *American Anthropologist,* XLIII (1941).

Cohen, Norm and Anne. "The Legendary Jimmie Tarleton." *Sing Out,* XVI (Sept. 1966).

Forten, Charlotte L. "Life on the Sea Islands." *Atlantic Monthly,* XIII (May 1864).

Green, Archie. "Dorsey Dixon: Minstrel of the Mills." *Sing Out,* XVI (July 1966).

Hudson, Arthur Palmer. "Folk Songs of the Southern Whites." *Culture in the South,* Ed. Couch, W. T. (Chapel Hill: 1935).

Means, C. E. "A Singular Literary Survival." *The Outlook* (Sept. 9, 1899).

Milling, Chapman J. "Delia Holmes: A Neglected Negro Ballad." *Southern Folklore Quarterly,* I (1937).

Parsons, Elsie Clews. "Folklore of the Sea Islands of South Carolina." *Memoirs of the American Folklore Society,* XVI (1923).

Redfield, Robert, et al. "Memorandum for the Study of Acculturation." *American Anthropologist,* XXXVIII (1938).

Seeger, Charles. "Factorial Analysis of the Song as an Approach to the Formulation of a Unitary Field Theory." *International Folk Music Journal,* XX (1968).

Smith, Reed. "The Ballad of Tradition." *Journal of American Folklore,* XLVI (1933).

———. "A Glance at the Ballad and Folksong Field." *Southern Folklore Quarterly,* I (1937).

———. "Gullah." *Bulletin of the University of South Carolina,* No. 190 (1926).

112   *Bibliography*

———. "The Traditional Ballad in America, 1933." *Journal of American Folklore*, XLVII (1934).

———. "The Traditional Ballad in America." *Journal of American Folklore*, L (1937).

Traum, Happy. "The Art of the Talking Blues." *Sing Out*, XV (Jan. 1966).

Work, John Wesley. "Introduction." *Folk Songs of the American Negro*, Ed. Work, Frederick J. (Nashville: 1907).

This book may be kept

FOURTE